The Freedom Machine

The Freedom Machine

An Unexpected Journey

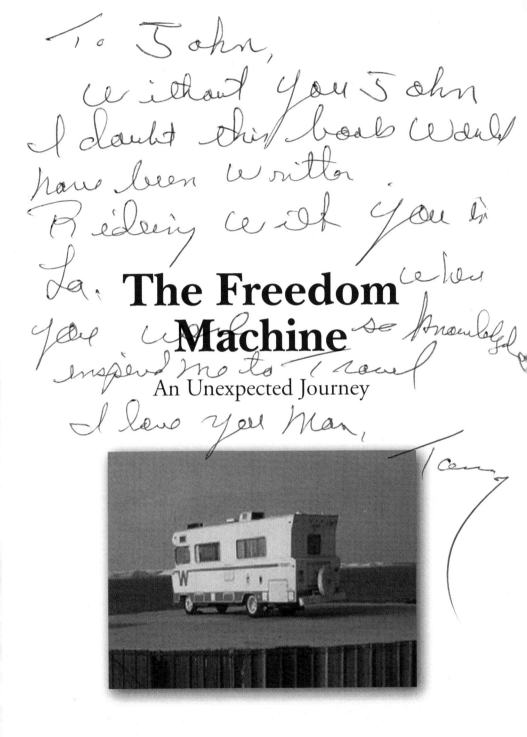

TOMMY HOWARD

Cover Photo: Tommy Howard
Cover Design: Scott Woldin
Interior Design: CreateSpace

First Edition: July/2016 Printed in the United States of America

ISBN: 1535326115
ISBN 13: 9781535326117

Praise For *The Freedom Machine*

If you own an RV, you should read this book; if you don't own an RV you should really read this book! Wayne Hand/Ocala, Fla.

Read it, loved it! David & Varley Twiddle/Busselton, Australia

I thoroughly enjoyed the story. Well told with original humor, and factual information. Joyful reading. Berlyn Temple/ Newport, NC

There are DIY books for just about everything but this is most definitely a DIY book for the mind, heart and soul. I couldn't put it down. Sorry I didn't have the courage to do what these two people did. Anne Dennis Murphy/Jacksonville, Fla.

Wonderful! It is written so clearly I can picture everything in my mind! What a culturally educational book! Luba Lemeny/Labrit, France

Educational! Exciting! Couple times there I thought they were not gong to make it! What a movie this would make! Gary Bach/Carolina Beach, NC

I would read three or four pages and then gaze off into space remembering and recalling those days in my past. The adventure, the excitement of waking up each morning to the wonders of what was going to happen next. And I cried and I mourned the death of my own hopes, dreams and expectations. Janna Sullivan/Ft. Collins, CO

A realistic view and cross section study of our south of the border Latino neighbors and how they actually feel about America. Revealing, inside exposure. Ligia Montalvo/Colorado Springs, CO

This book is dedicated to my mom, who always wanted to travel.

My name is Tommy Howard. At the age of 34, I sold most of what I owned, climbed into what Daddy called my Gypsy Shack motorhome, put him and all of Newport, North Carolina, in my rear view mirror and did not look back. I'm pretty sure that if I had looked back I would have turned to a pillar of salt and the unimagined life waiting for me would still be waiting. This is my story. Enjoy the ride.

Wherever you are in a motorhome, when you turn the engine off – you're home.
Tommy

Mom, we are not searching for happiness; we're taking it with us. Linda

Prologue:
Living In A Poem

*L*iving in North Carolina is like living in a poem.

That was a song written by a fella in Hollywood who had never felt a grain of North Carolina dirt between his toes. If you can tell me what rhymes with gators, copperheads, snuff dipping and possums I will admit that maybe that Hollywood fella might have been onto something.

Truth is, Newport, North Carolina has dirt roads that don't rhyme with anything, tobacco farms that don't rhyme with anything and one traffic signal that don't have rhyme or reason for even being there.

Most of the farmers living around Newport were as poor as rats and destined to stay poor till they passed. I'll tell you right here and now, if there's a cover charge to get into heaven, no farmer from Newport, North Carolina is ever getting in.

We do have a way with sweet potatoes, though. We know more about them than Sears knows about Roebuck. We have to. It's our state vegetable.

Tommy Howard

You want to know the real meaning of Southern Comfort, toss a few sweet potatoes into the fire, wait awhile, fish 'em out, pour on the butter and salt and dig in.

Now *that's* poetry!

So, there I was, living' in the middle of a poem. Me, my three brothers and a mama that tried and a daddy that didn't. We never saw him much. He had more "important" things to do than to socialize with the likes of us. Namely drink like a man on fire.

He was the General and to his way of thinking the General never fraternized with the troops. We were to be seen – long as we were seen working - and never heard. His allegiance and social life was anywhere but home.

If we were keeping score, as a father, he scored a 0. As a bully slave master, he scored 100.

That man worked us six days a week feeding chickens, shucking corn for the mules, milking the cow and, when we were old enough, planting, growing, cutting, picking, drying tobacco – which never made no sense to me because how do you make money growing something for 53 cents a pound and then selling it for 47 cents a pound?

But question the man and you were likely to find your skull butting heads with the business end of a two-by-four or a hubcap or anything else within reach.

I call them days the Glory Days because whenever Daddy *was* around, any one of us was within an inch or two of going home to Glory.

It was college that saved me.

The Freedom Machine

I started out failing the entrance exam at UNC Chapel Hill then went on down to Greenville and failed the entrance exam at East Carolina University. Hell, I didn't have but a 10th grade education. Wasn't my teachers' fault. Lord knows they tried but putting learning into a head as hard as a cue ball is about as easy as feeding a dead cat. I *could* blame a lot of that on my daddy. Doing homework ranked last on the list of chores that needed doing.

If we were keeping score on that account, it would be homework 0, chores 100.

But …

Being as how I was the only one of 54 first cousins to ever step foot on a college campus and being as how I did not want to hear the other 53 *and* Daddy say, "Flunked out like everybody knew you would." I tracked down the fella that ran the place - Dean Holt - and pestered him like a horn fly pesters a cow's belly. He finally gave in and, "against my better judgment" let me in. He probably figured I'd drop right back out as soon as I saw how tough it was. But I dug in, stayed the whole four years *and* graduated.

Still had to go work the farm every weekend, though. No room for argument there.

My college degree and me went home and got talked into trying to save Daddy's construction business, which was $180,000 in the hole. It took six years of my life and probably ten years *off* my life.

Still, I did it. And I got to thinking; if I could save *that* business, how hard would it be to *build* another one? After all I went through trying to save my daddy's butt, anything else would be a piece of cake.

Just not in Newport.

Tommy Howard

I was done living in that particular poem so, like a cowboy backing out of a saloon with both guns blazing, I headed back to Greenville.

By the time I was 34 I had five different businesses, every one of them booming.

Business number five was the one that changed my life.

The company was called U-Ren-Co. We rented things. One day the manager comes to me and says:

"I got people – lots of 'em - asking if we have an RV to rent out. Think we should get one?"

"Do the math. If we come out on top then go get us an RV."

Next thing I know, there's a shiny new Winnebago 24 Class A setting out on the lot. We didn't make enough off it to buy new suits but we didn't lose our shirts, either.

One weekend when that Winnebago wasn't being rented out I thought I'd take it out on my own, maybe drive it around the Outer Banks for a day or two.

Poetry!

Everything changed.

Part One

THE FREEDOM MACHINE

One

*W*hy am I here?

How many times have you asked yourself (or God) that question?

I thought maybe I'd find the answer in *Handbook To Higher Consciousness*, a book that, according to Amazon, *has helped countless people experience dramatic changes in their lives from the time they begin applying the simple, effective techniques.* I read that book from cover to cover a hundred times and got more out of it than any book I ever opened in college. Git right down to it, it was genuine fish 'n tater talk. I bet there were nights I slept with it under my pillow.

But I still didn't know why I was here.

So, one day in 1976 I decided to go meet the man who wrote the book. His name was Ken Keyes Jr. and he was all the way out in Berkley, California. I was pretty certain he wouldn't be coming southeast so my blue-eyed, blond best friend and future wife, Linda, and me got into that Winnebago and headed west.

I was not prepared for what was waiting.

Two

I wanted to shake the hand of the man who wrote the book that I had carried with me for years and still carry to this day. The same book I have bought as a gift to at least 300 people. Just wanted to shake the man's hand.

Wasn't going to happen.

Because at age 25, Ken Keyes Jr. got himself blindsided by polio. Woke up one day and couldn't move his legs or his hands.

It got worse.

The paralysis turned into quadriplegia so bad he could not even turn himself over in bed. So what did he do? He went ahead and invented a switch-activated power bed that would turn his body over *for* him. He said he "*began to develop the feeling that I did not have to be so totally dependent on other people*" and "*still wanted to feel that I was a capable and lovable person.*" That was when he moved from his old wheelchair into a lever-controlled electric wheelchair.

I heard that some reporter fella started asking questions, trying to make Mr. Keyes admit to being angry and bitter and having a chip on his shoulder. Sure, he could go ahead and write them self-help books till the cows came home but underneath it all:

"Aren't you really just an unhappy, crippled man, mad at the world?"

The Freedom Machine

He looked that reporter in the eye and said:

"We always have enough to be happy if we are enjoying what we *do* have and not worrying about what we *don't* have."

Whew!

Linda and me got all the way to Arizona before I could snap out of what I was calling the Ken Keyes Experience

Then came the Grand Canyon Experience.

Three

"To quote a friend of mine, Wes Price, 'If that ain't the biggest hole in the ground *anywhere*, grits ain't groceries'."

"You're kidding, right?" asked the old fella standing next to me.

"Hell, no, I'm not kidding! I have heard all about the Grand Canyon being big, but this is ridiculous! I been in road construction, digging and filling for years, but surely never saw such a deep crack in the earth as this!"

"Well, if you think this is big, wait till you see the Grand Canyon."

"Wait, what? This *is* the Grand Canyon, is it not?"

"Oh no, this is just a fissure, a crack in the ground."

"A crack in the ground? You aren't lying to me now, are you?"

"No, son, I'm not. The Grand Canyon is that way." He pointed south.

"Well, thank you, mister! I am sure glad I didn't turn around right here and go back to North Carolina thinking I had seen The Grand Canyon!"

Right about then, Linda came walking up, holding the camera.

The Freedom Machine

"Sweetheart, this is *not* the Grand Canyon, it's just a crack in the ground. Put the camera away, jump back in the Winnebago and let's head south."

We reached the South Rim right around sunset, just in time to see a sight like to take your breath away.

Beyond imagination.

I left the camera in the camper. It wouldn't do me any good out there. Wouldn't do anyone any good. You could take a thousand pictures of that Grand Canyon and not one of 'em would look anything like what it really was. You could put it on TV and you still wouldn't get the whole picture.

Beyond imagination.

Standing there looking out at it, I heard a voice inside my head telling me, "You've got to spend some time here, Tommy boy."

We checked into a campsite pretty close to the South Rim and went to what they called a Campfire Slideshow put on by the ranger.

"The Grand Canyon is 277 miles long, up to 18 miles wide and more than a mile deep." were his opening words.

I was all ears.

"So when you look down, down, down toward the bottom, what you might think is a bird flying could be an airplane. That ribbon you see at the bottom of the Canyon is the Colorado River. It started in Wyoming, ran all the way down to Mexico and emptied into the Sea of Cortez. It ran for millions of years right through this area until, gradually, deep formations caused the area to start swelling up. That didn't stop the river though. The more it would swell the more it would cut - a few centimeters a year for four and a half million years."

Now, if that wasn't an example of time, the Ranger went on to explain in more detail the time structure. This is important because this is where you can actually *see* time.

"Lets make a twenty-four hour time comparison between the time the earth was born, about 4 to 5 billion years ago, to the age of the Canyon. Let's start at 12:00 midnight and start looking for anything to happen about breakfast time, lunchtime, dinnertime. No Grand Canyon. Just before you give it up and say good night, at four minutes to midnight the Canyon begins to form. Next thing you know, four or five million years have slipped by and look at that ... The Grand Canyon!"

Beyond imagination.

Round about midnight, sitting fifteen feet or so from the rim of the canyon, looking up at stars so close I felt I could touch them, watching the moon looking down at four and a half million years of nature's handiwork, I saw it for myself.

I *saw* time!

I did a little math of my own. It worked out that my life would be the last fifth of a second before midnight. Had to be a message in there.

Looking up into the vastness of space and then down into the vastness of The Grand Canyon, I knew right then, my life was changed forever. I might look the same and walk the same, but I was a different man. I had looked *time* straight in the eyes.

"Nature will tell you something, if you let it. It is called *quietly listening.*"

The Freedom Machine

The words came gently to me. I was getting a message. Something like, *life is short, and the world is round. What do you want to do with the rest of your short life?*

I looked east to where my five businesses and security waited. I had worked long and hard to found and develop those businesses and they were all up and running, successfully. I knew what was waiting; make more money, spend more money; more money, more employees, more bank meetings, more lawsuits, more … business. Your business gets bigger, your problems get bigger.

Sure, just like you, I'd heard it a thousand times:

One of these days, when I get to be sixty-five, I 'm going to retire and Martha and me are going to sit back and enjoy the fruits of our labor.

Just one problem there, Charlie Brown.

Who says you and Martha are going to *get* to be sixty-five, and if you do, what is your health situation going to be?

I looked west.

I could *feel* the call of adventure and curiosity. It was real. Yeah, **real** is the best word I could come up with. I don't recall where I first heard this but I do remember someone saying it:

The only thing that separates man from animals is, **we have a choice**.

I looked further west.

And heard Ken Keyes Jr. talking to me all the way from Berkley:

People who postpone happiness are like children who try chasing rainbows in an effort to find the pot of gold at the rainbow's end. Your life will never be fulfilled until you are happy here and now.

Nature will tell you something if you listen close enough.

Now all I had to do was tell Daddy.

Four

"Daddy, I have decided to sell my business and do some traveling.

"Which business you gonna sell?"

"All of them!"

"And just travel?"

Silence.

The scary kind.

"Thought it over pretty good and it's what I want to do."

"Thought it over, have ya?"

He wasn't looking at me; he was staring into his coffee cup.

"You mean to tell me, as much money as your mammy and me spent sendin' you through that college and getting you educated, you are going to repay us by gettin' in that damn Gypsy Shack motorhome and start running up and down the road?"

Tommy Howard

At least he didn't ask me where I was planning to go cause since I had no idea, that could have been awkward.

"Where do you plan to go, Tommy?"

Oh, Mama.

Silence.

The awkward kind.

"Don't know."

"You sure as hell don't," Daddy said, with less than a kind look in his eyes and at that particular moment all I could see were his eyes. See he had this habit of pouring his coffee onto a saucer and slurping it into his mouth off the saucer. Said it saved time and he had "more important things to do than sit around drinking coffee."

I couldn't explain it any better and one thing for sure, I knew they would understand a whole lot less if I tried to explain the Grand Canyon Experience and what was *really* behind such a change in direction. I'm still not sure I even can explain that to myself.

I just knew that somewhere, someway, there was something strange and strong pulling me, assuring me. Without one clue of doubt, there was more to life than what I had; something more important than all the money and success any business could ever offer. I didn't know *what* it was, but I was damn sure of one thing - it was there, it was real, and I was going find it.

I wanted to say to my daddy something I heard Henry David Thoreau had said … *Most men lead lives of quiet desperation and go to the grave with the song still in them* … but instead I just looked into his eyes hovering over that saucer and said, "I'll send postcards" and got the heck out of Dodge.

Five

Bobby Eason was a straight-A student that made the Dean's List every year. I must have looked to him like a straight A out of the country bumpkin that couldn't make a list if it was spelled out in Alpha Bits.

But he took a liking to me.

I will tell anyone anywhere any time – Bobby Eason is the reason I made it through college and the reason why all five of my businesses were making money. How can you lose with a man that passed his CPA exam first time around? He was also my best friend. Still is.

"Hey Bobby, how are you, Anne and Michael doing?"

"Pretty good there, Tommy. What's up?"

"Are you sitting down, Mr. CPA man?"

"I'm always sitting down. Isn't that what accountants do?"

"If you say so. Look, I need you to figure out what I could sell my businesses for."

"Which one?"

"All of 'em."

Silence.

The "What have you been smoking?" kind.

"Bobby?"

"I'm here. Just let me put my glasses back on and get up off the floor. Umm …when do you want to do all this selling?"

"Soon as you can get it done. I want to give my employees first shot at buying. I'll finance the balance. I don't need much down."

"Are you sure everything is okay, Tommy? I mean, man, you worked hard putting these business together, and they are just taking off. Now is not the time to sell. They'll each be worth a fortune if you hold on just a little longer!"

"Bobby, I have never been any surer of anything else in my life! How about you work out the details, cause I need to be moving on. Got the Winnebago half packed already."

He had everything sold in sixty days.

Six

Linda is tall, blond and beautiful with a good sense of humor. She is also the most intelligent woman I know, with a Masters in Special Education. Not a bad traveling partner, wouldn't you say?

"Okay, I have resigned my teaching job and signed on. Which way are we headed and where are we going?"

"Doesn't matter which way or where. It is where we end up that counts."

"Where we end up?"

"Yeah. We can be headed one place and end up in another, but we got to head somewhere to end up somewhere else. Does that make sense?"

"In your mind, I'm sure it does."

"Darlin', I gave my watch away, I disconnected the speedometer and I removed all the clocks. If we don't know how fast we are going or how far we have traveled, or what time it is, we can't be late or early. So if someone asks what time it is, it is *now* and if they want to know where we are we're *here*. Now does that make any sense to you?"

"Tommy, I gave up a good teaching career and will follow you to the end, but can I get a little more than that? I mean... my mother ... I have to tell her more than that."

"Tell her we are in pursuit of happiness, looking to find out who we are and why we are here."

"That won't work. What else have you got?"

"How about the world is round and life is short!"

Silence.

The "Get serious" kind.

"Closest I can come to what this is all about is the universe is sending messages we need for our growth. We are going in search of the answer every single human being on the earth needs to know and the answer lies in the pursuit. We will mail it to your mother soon as we find it."

"Sounds more like Einstein's Theory on the Fabric of Time to me than anything else."

"Works for me. Now hop in, shut the door and let's go. We don't want to be late, we don't want to be early but we also don't want to be standing still. Look, I even got us a road map. I just don't know which direction to point us in. Facts are, if we live a thousand years and travel every day, we won't even scratch the surface of places to go, people to meet, and things to do, so lets remember that, no matter which direction."

"One thing for sure, Tommy Boy, we can't go very far east before we drive into Atlantic Ocean and we don't want to go South. We could go west but we did that last year and I don't think the Grand Canyon has changed much so … it's the perfect time to see Autumn in New England."

Seven

O n the road ...

Nice campgrounds right outside Washington, DC. Can drive the Winnebago to a terminal, park it, catch the subway to The Smithsonian. Who says you can't do city stuff in a motor home? They tell us it would take six years to go through the whole complex. We'll give it a week. **From Tommy's Journal**

Really hard to believe how much wilderness we're surrounded by right outside DC. Shooting stars, serenity, safety and good neighbors. We'll bookmark this campground for sure. **From Linda's Diary**

"New York is on the way to New England and there's a campground just few blocks from the Holland Tunnel for $37.00 a day. It overlooks Manhattan Island and the shuttle comes by hourly to take us into town."

"I hear there are people who are born, live and die in New York and never leave for anything."

"Big interesting place, alright, but just a dot the size a pencil would leave on any average size globe. Kinda puts things in perspective."

"That's worth remembering every single day. Oh, Lord, Tommy, I'm starting to think like you!"

"And I like the way you think."

Mystic, Connecticut. Never heard of it, but not a mile out the way. How quaint. Lots of history here … maritime museum, tall ships. I'm a teacher (retired). I thrive on learning about and experiencing new places. **From Linda's Diary**

"Wow, Tommy, look at these colors! It's like we're camped right in the middle of a box of crayons! I bet they put pictures of this in all the hotel rooms in Vermont."

"Fella a couple of spots down the campground says if we think autumn in New England is something we oughta go to Nova Scotia, take a spin around cape Breton Island."

"Canada?"

"Uh-huh. Said we should also go down around the Bay of Fundy in New Brunswick. Says they got the highest tides in the world there … up to 55 feet. Gotta run like hell when the tide starts coming in. People been killed who couldn't run fast enough!"

"So, we're going to Canada?"

"If you can't trust your neighbor in an RV camp, who *can* you trust?"

Reversing Falls, New Brunswick. The tide pushes the river back upstream and then in the afternoon the river pushes the tide back the other way toward the bay. We had lunch, took a nap and had a great vantage point of view to see it actually go two ways. **From Tommy's Journal**

On the road again.

The Freedom Machine

Glenholme, Nova Scotia, Auld's Cove, Nova Scotia, Cape Breton national Park, Indian Brook, New Glasgow. Montreal, Quebec, Sault Ste. Marie, Ontario.

Niagara Falls! Everything we thought it would be and more. Canadians say their side is the prettiest. Americans say theirs is prettiest. I say both sides are right. All that water falling is mind blowing. Can you imagine some fool tucking himself into a barrel and going over? **From Tommy's Journal**

We kept going on across Canada till the weather didn't suit our summer clothes anymore and then headed south, through North Dakota and into the Black Hills of South Dakota. They aren't really black, they just look black from a distance cause they're all covered in trees and the trees are what make 'em look black.

"Would you look at that? That is a marvel of engineering!"

"It says here that the carving started in 1927 and wasn't finished till 1941."

"Took 'em all that time and effort to carve them boys into Mount Rushmore and it takes us no effort at all to stand here and look at their handiwork. Should we feel guilty? According to the Grand Canyon way of thinking, no, we should not feel guilty, we should enjoy their effort."

The weather kept getting colder so we popped a few postcards in the mail to the folks back home (I have often wondered if they took the time and interest to look at them or just threw them in the trash when they seen they was from us traveling gypsies) and pointed ourselves in the direction of San Diego, the warmest place in the country right then according to the TV news. Linda wanted to know how far out of the way would it be if we went through Las Vegas?

Hey, Las Vegas is nice. Cheapest campgrounds in the USA, if you don't gamble. And not being gamblers, we had plenty to do. Had our dress-ups with us so we got to a different show every night. Slept all day. Lived the high life, staying at the Thunderbird, the MGM. The Sands and The Tropicana. Parking lots, that is.
From Tommy's Journal

Las Vegas. Tom Jones, Robert Goulet, Foster Brooks, Joan Rivers, MacDavis, Roy Clark, Barbara Fairchild, George Foreman, Howard Cosell. **From Linda's Diary**

I knew a girl who used to say, "A little powder, a little paint can make a lady what she ain't". It wasn't long before Las Vegas got to be that way. The powder and the paint began to wear off and the highway started calling.

Not sure how we ended up in Death Valley but there we were. A Ranger fella surmised to us that when God made the world, He tossed all the left overs into Death Valley. I have to admit, it is a particularly peculiar place.

Take the Devil's Golf Course and take my word for it - only the devil could play golf on that piece of chopped up land. I mean a duck would have trouble even flying over such a choppy mess. I can't imagine what people thought the first time they discovered it. Acres and acres of tons and tons of salt that maybe was flat at one time or another but then started to buckle and push up till it looked like one of those caves full of stalagmites and stalactites.

We spent most of the day there, hiking, eating, napping and, in between, wondering why we were the only two people for miles around.

Where was everybody?

The Freedom Machine

"Tommy, it's the end of November. Most people are still trying to walk off their Thanksgiving turkey and get ready for Christmas. Last thing on their mind is taking a run out to Death Valley to watch some daffy duck lose his tail feathers trying to fly over the damn Devil's Golf Course."

She had a point.

We went home for Christmas. Watched Daddy drink coffee from the saucer. Took Mama to the see the doctor. She told everyone in the waiting room I was her son … the one without a job. Seems it just kept getting easier and easier to put my hometown in my rear view mirror. And I had the Freedom Machine to do it.

By the time the New Year's confetti had been swept up off the streets, Linda and me were back in California.

Free camping every night at Sea World. These San Diego folks got it going pretty good. **From Tommy's Journal**

Parked for weeks right on the beach. Never had a clue of what kind of crazy was going to come whizzing by on roller blades. **From Linda's Diary**

"Linda, do you know it's only about 20 miles from right here in San Diego to the Mexico border?"

"That's one place we'll never go."

Part Two

MEXICO

Eight

"Mexico? Mexican Insurance? No thanks. Heard too many strange stories about south of the border." I'm talking with a man from the San Diego Chamber of Commerce.

"No, it's not like that anymore. They have Green Angels patrolling."

"I don't care what color they are. Not interested."

"Have you ever touched a whale?"

"Never even seen one."

There's a little Old Mexico town along the Baja Peninsula famous for whale experiences. The whales will actually bring their babies up close and personal for you to have a look."

"Really?" He has my attention now.

"Really. The town is called Mulege - only six hundred or so miles from right where you're standing."

I looked over at Linda.

"Not me. I'd rather stay here and dodge roller blades."

"Tell you what – I'll make you a promise. Let's buy a couple weeks' worth of insurance and go see the whales but I promise you, the very second you feel even the tiniest bit uncomfortable, I'll turn the Freedom Machine around and come right back to the USA.

Nine

"Lin, you sure we should rent this locker? Gotta pay a month just for two weeks!" Can't talk him down."

"Yeah, I'd feel better. We've got our snow skis, our TV, all our stuff. Who knows? If we get out of Mexico alive, that may be all we have left."

Tijuana, Saint Lomas, San Quintin, Parador Punta Prieta, Guerrero Negro, Mulege. Made it. Whew! **From Linda's Diary**

Roads not too bad if you drive slow and who's in a hurry anyway? Stayed in campgrounds all the way to Mulege. Not used to that but Linda felt safer. Mexico's starting to grow on her though. Hope the whales will seal the deal. **From Tommy's Journal**

"Oh yeah, look at that! This was worth the trip right here! These whales have traveled all the way from Alaska!"

"My God, Tommy, they are huge!"

We were whale watching from the comfort of our living room. That's the thing about owning a Freedom Machine - it's your living room, your bedroom, hotel, car, restaurant and home.

Tommy Howard

Sometimes, we could see three, four and five waterspouts at a time and then, when got on top of the Winnebago and put the binoculars on the baby whales … wow! Those babies had to weigh about three thousand pounds and were about as cute as a three thousand pound kid can be!

Standing there looking out at those magnificent beasts got me to thinking about all them whale hunters. How could anybody think they had the right to take the life of such a wonderful being? It about broke my heart.

I was so close (and getting closer) to a couple of 'em that they turned and looked at me standing there on the dock I wanted to get right in the ocean with them.

"I made eye contact, Linda! Oh my God, we were looking right at each other!"

Believe it or not, that mama whale actually turned around and did it again! Looked me square in the eyes. Now we were getting somewhere!

"That whale is trying to talk to me! Look real close; you'll see what I mean. Shades of the Grand Canyon! These whales are trying to talk to us, Linda! Maybe they have the answers we're looking for?"

I was convinced that their oh so slow movements were a message, a beckoning for us to follow them. Mentally, I mean, not physically. These giants were wise beyond their years and I knew in my soul they knew more than any man, woman or child. What's more, I knew they were trying to send me the messages I needed for my growth toward higher consciousness.

"Don't you think it time we leave, Tommy?" Our two weeks insurance is almost up."

"Sorry, hon, I'm just really connecting with these creatures. They know something we don't."

I watched them all day for days and all night even when I couldn't see them, I could feel them trying and trying to send me a message.

I never got it.

With a sadness I had never known, I pulled the Winnie slowly, slowly out of the campground.

I did not want to leave. Couldn't bring myself to go faster than fifteen miles per hour cause every hour put me another hour further from the whales. They were locked in my head and I could not get them out.

"I am telling you, Linda, they had the answer. They gave it to me. I just can't put it into words. Let's turn around and go back. I tell you I am close on it! "

"Tommy, we have to go. The whales have been coming here for millions of years, so maybe if the universe doesn't answer you soon, we can come back and you can talk to your whales."

Pushed it up to twenty miles an hour. Best I could do just then.
"If you kick it up a few miles per hour we should make it back to the states by the time the insurance expires."

"Well, Lin, I was just thinking. We are already half way down this peninsula; lets keep going on down to to Cabo San Lucas. Maybe we can pick up another couple weeks insurance in La Paz?"

Ten

So many people think Mexico, in particular the border towns, is not a safe place to travel. Use ordinary everyday caution and Mexico is as safe as the U.S. – safer in a lot of places.

Take the Baja Peninsula.

Safe as Solomon's birds.

Half the people you meet are Americans and because of that the campground owners all speak English. Prices are about half what American campgrounds cost. Lots of grocery stores, well stocked and clean. When you get right down to it, the Baja Peninsula is a pretty good way to "break in" a different country and culture, have yourself a real educational see and do and share and such, all from the comfort of your living room on wheels. You might not want to leave.

Ever.

We met a couple, Chris and Bonnie. They ventured into Mexico to spend a couple weeks vacation. Fell in love with the country and each other all over again. They got home, found they could rent their house out for $400 per month more than their mortgage, go on back to Mexico in their RV and live pretty nicely on that little bit of extra income. They might not have the luxuries of home, but they would have a life of freedom in a Freedom Machine.

The Freedom Machine

They made their choice and it worked for them. They were on their fourth year south of the border.

We met a New York City detective who just couldn't go back to running in crooks and killers in a big, dirty city when he could be running on the beaches in the gentle, laid back lifestyle of Mexico. He was on his fifteenth year.

We met a pharmacist who just couldn't go back to Chicago. He parked his VW camper right there in Mexico and didn't move it for twenty-two years. The trees grew up around the camper till it looked like a nest in a forest. It was there to stay. So was the pharmacist. I have the pictures to prove it.

Give Mexico a try. You might not want to leave.

Ever.

Eleven

The Freedom Machine was headed to a sleepy little seaport called La Paz when we passed by a dirt road we couldn't pass up. It dead-ended at an RV camp looking out on the Sea of Cortez. The fishing was good, the campers were friendly and the price was right - $5 a week. A Mexican fella came by once a week to collect from everyone. Still not sure if he owned the campground. We stayed a week. Got our $5 worth.

La Paz means "Peace" in Spanish and that's exactly what you're gonna get. You're a thousand miles from the dirt and dust of Tijuana and a million miles from any kind of bad weather.

"Hey. Lin, we can take a 24-hour ferry ride from La Paz over to Mazatlan and head back home on a different route. Only problem is we'll miss the whales. I sincerely hate that."

Semana Santa (Easter Week) in Mazatlan involves music. One afternoon I saw five mariachi bands singing and grinning their way down the beach. A lot of dancing, a lot of eating and not a lot of sleep. Linda went on a fruit diet for eight days after spending a little too much time at a clam stand. **From Tommy's Journal**

The plan was to head north from Mazatlan but that ol' Freedom Machine had a mysterious mind of its own and we found ourselves in a nice little campground in San Blas, about 175 miles **south** of Mazatlan. That's where we met Dennis, the Elvis freak.

The Freedom Machine

"Where are you all headed when you leave outta here?" Elvis wanted to know.

"We're thinking maybe we'll head on over to Puerto Vallarta. How about you?"

"I was going the same way. What's chances of hitching a ride?"

"Sure, leaving in the morning. Come knock on our door but I'm warning you, we travel slow."

"Not a problem. Nobody travels slower'n me and this ol' guitar."

Sure enough, Dennis the Elvis was knocking on our door at the crack of dawn. He was a nice enough fella but the mistake he made was asking us what we thought of Matanchen Bay.

Twelve

"What did y'all think of Matanchen Bay?"

"What's Matanchen Bay?"

"Best word I can find to describe it is 'wow!' We'll be goin' right by the road that leads into there 'cept it's sandy and rough. I don't know if you can get this motor home in there or not."

"Don't you worry about that. I grew up driving on sandy and narrow roads."

Dennis the Elvis was right.

Wow!

Surfer's paradise," said Dennis the Elvis. Tons of California surfers live here. Once it had the longest surfable wave in the world."

"Seriously?"

"Yes, sir. It's in the Guinness Book of World Records."

"Makes me feel like I'm standing on holy ground."

The Freedom Machine

"If you were Huichol, you *would* be standing on holy ground."

I turned around to see this big ol' surfer boy walking up to us wearing nothing but a shirt and a bathing suit. I learned later that his total wardrobe consisted of two shirts and three bathing suits. I never saw him wear anything else.

"Don Jones," he said, smiling and sticking his hand out. He was tall, blond, bearded and had muscle on top of muscle. I glanced over to see if Linda was noticing him. She was.

"Don't see many … let me rephrase that … don't see *any* Winnebago's around here. I know a good place you can park if you're staying the night. It's in back of a palapa. Be a little like having a Winnebago with a front porch – and there's no charge."

"Can't see why not," I told him. "And you can't beat the price."

"Sounds good to me, "says Dennis the Elvis. "I'll just string my hammock right next to it."

A palapa is an open-sided dwelling with a thatched roof made of dried palm eaves. Slide your Winnebago in behind it and you do indeed have front porch.

"This is a great place Don, Thanks for the tip. How long you been here?'

"About five years. I rent surfboards and get supplies to other surfers.
One thing I like about this place is the neighbors. I mean I look out the window and feel like we are part of the tribe."

"Tribe?"

"Have you heard of the Huichol Indians?"

"No." said Linda.

"The Huichol are seriously spiritual. You can see how spiritual in their yarn paintings and beadwork. They have four gods but the god that inspires their art is the peyote cactus."

"Peyote? That's illegal, isn't it?"

"To the Huichol, it's holy. Peyote is the god that enables them to walk and talk with their other gods. Just like the Muslim's lifelong desire to make his pilgrimage to Mecca, it is the ambition and plight of the Huichol Indian to take part in the annual pilgrimage to get their necessary supplies of peyote."

"Pilgrimage?"

"Yes indeed, Linda. They live in the Sierra Madre Mountains. Hard places to get to. Mystic soothsayers prefer not to live in villages, but they do come down every October to send off the bravest of the warriors to capture Peyote.

"These warriors have to go through a purifying ritual for three days. On the fourth day they sit around a fire and confess their adulteries, knotting a string once for each lapse and then throwing that string into the fire. Fully absolved and purified, eight to ten of them are then sent forth to find Peyote. One warrior who's done this before remains behind to maintain contact between them and the gods. He knows the roads and prays constantly. He knows the journey will take forty-three days and he has a string with forty-three knots and unties one each day until they return. The leader of the expedition has a similar string, so, in a strange way, they are communicating.

"It is important to see the reindeer in their travels because this means that they are in contact with the gods and their communication is sacred.

"On the 19th day they arrive to the sacred place where the peyote was created and found. They pray to be saved from the madness, a real danger during the next few days when they will be gorging themselves on the peyote. They all crouch into a stalking position, slowly creeping up on the plant. Then two of the more experienced warriors separate about thirty feet or so and shoot their arrows. They must cross exactly behind the cactus to block the retreat of the spirit of the peyote god. Then they most diligently and with bowed heads pick only choice branches, careful not to damage the plant or make it angry.

"Another necessary part of the ritual is to rub the yellow juices over their entire bodies on a daily bases as they return home. They reach home on the 43rd day, utterly exhausted and barely recognizable."

"Man," says me. "That is one tough pilgrimage!"

"Not over yet. They are now obliged to get very drunk. The Huichol believe it is dangerous to have anything to do with the gods when completely sober.

"They are now stocked up with a twelve month supply of peyote and their land is virtually insured against drought for the coming year. The cycle of planting and harvesting can begin.

"First there is an extended Peyote festival, assuring unmeasured wealth when the people eat the newly collected cactus. They live in a state of exaltation, not intoxication, as with alcohol. In fact their physical balance is better than usual and they are easily able to endure hunger, thirst and fatigue. This euphoric state puts them into a higher consciousness and they believe they are actually walking and talking with the gods, receiving wisdom and messages to assure them of good judgment."

"Wow! That was like the best bedtime story I ever heard and it ain't even dark yet!" says Dennis the Elvis.

"You ever tried it Don?"

"I'll just say it gives strength and depth to thinking like you can' t explain and, according to legend, (He winked at us) you have eyesight sharper than an owl at midnight."

"Well," says Dennis the Elvis, scratching his chin and looking around. "Lookee there, it *is* starting to get dark."

Thirteen

Matanchen Bay is written up in travel books as somewhere you have to *beware of the many biting mosquitoes and insects.* Not true but it keeps the tourists away and the locals love it. We loved it, too. Never saw so many crabs and bats before in my life but still not a bad place to hang around awhile.

Lizards, iguanas, fresh fish for dinner, surfing and last night a cow wandered into the palapa. A tropical paradise! **From Linda's Diary**

Natural hot springs, banana trees, date palms, sand pipers, pelicans, coconuts, mangos, melons and skinny-dipping in the bay surrounded by thousands of fish! Why would anyone want to be anywhere else? **From Linda's Diary**

"When you all going on to Puerto Vallarta?" asked Dennis the Elvis.

"Lin and I were just talking about that this morning and we think maybe a month or so."

" A month?"

"Give or take a day or two."

"Well now, you all told me you traveled slow when I signed on but only three miles in a month? That's a little slower than I had imagined. Think maybe I'll be heading out."

39

"Well, alright then. Adios, Elvis. Maybe we will run into ya somewhere down the road."

We never saw or heard from him again.

Red Tide tonight. Looks like sparks flying on the water. They tell me this is not good for marine life. Awful pretty though. Then again, so was Jezebel I hear. **From Tommy's Journal**

Antonio, one of the local fellas, says if you grab a live electrical wire it's a sure cure for nausea and hiccups, which he says he suffers from after smoking his peyote. I'm gonna have to take his word for that. **From Tommy's Journal**

"Don, tell me the truth. You ever tried peyote?"

"Yes, I did, once. Wouldn't ever do it again."

"How did it make you feel, I mean could you surf? Could you catch a wave?"

"Hey, man, it was like I *was* the wave!"

"Did you find yourself walking and talking with the gods?"

"I did."

After Don left, I had the urge to climb up on top of the motor home, much as I had climbed up on top of the tobacco barn in my youth, and sit and stare out into space and let my imagination have at it.

Beautiful night. A million stars. If we hadn't packed our life into the Freedom Machine and taken off I'd probably be sitting somewhere looking up at streetlights. I wished right then that I could convince everyone everywhere to get their own Freedom Machine and experience moments like what I was experiencing before life passes them by and it's too late.

A tranquility began to settle over me. I opened all my receptors, feeling like I could walk and talk with God. No peyote necessary.

So quiet.

"Who am I? Why am I here? What does the future hold?" I whispered to the sky.

I'll never know where it came from, but it was so clear that I wrote it down soon as I climbed down from the Winnebago.

"You are the essence of God, my child of the universe. You are of and from the universe. You are made up of the same components from which the stars ascend.

The universe is of time, billions of years in the creation. You are of the same origin, so you must allow the wisdom to unfold as the universe has and ever continues to do. The universe is still expanding and growing; so must you.

Your knowledge will come in time, if you allow the eternal now spirit that now dwells within you to dwell in peace.

There are steps and procedures. They cannot be rushed. The final solution will be yours. It can be explained as a conscious growth expanding toward higher consciousness. The steps of procedure will come, but only in silence and serenity.

You must dwell in a higher form of consciousness in order to get the messages you will need for your growth. You cannot go to the final solution, cosmic consciousness, directly.

You will take the necessary steps in time and time alone. In truth, you already have it, but don't know how to deal with it. Be Patient."

And it was gone, as quickly as it had come.

I knew for the first time the answer I was seeking would, in fact, be revealed. And I knew one thing for sure. I could not have had such an experience in any hotel or resort in the world. I had had a message in the Grand Canyon that nature will tell you something if you let it.

So let it.

Tranquility: being one with the grace, peace and space of the nature of the universe.

For a brief moment, I was back in the Grand Canyon, seeing time again, but now I was able to hitch a ride. What a universe! What a gift!

Life.

Precious and fragile.

And don't forget to smell the flowers.

That night would live forever, last forever.

Over a month had passed since we pulled in for a look around Matanchen Bay. A month I'll never forget. A spot on the map I'll never forget. I hope to get back there one day but on that day, the morning after that amazing night before, I knew it was time to move on. Ever have that feeling? You wake up one day and you know that you know.

We said goodbye to Don Jones, promised we'd hook up again in another lifetime and pointed the Freedom Machine in the direction of Puerto Vallarta.

Fourteen

Beautiful place, Puerto Vallarta. A little too touristy for us but we did take a nice boat ride over to Yelapa, a little fishing village off the coast and ate some good Mexican food in a quaint restaurant. Yeah, quaint is about good as I can do.

Back in Puerto Vallarta we tried parasailing and Linda went vegetarian. Neither one of those things had anything to do with the other.

Things I learned in Puerto Vallarta: Rub lemon or lime on mosquito bites, do not drink too many Coco Locos, Mexican women wash clothes in the river and rub them on rocks, Mexican women are beautiful and Mexican men are 100% macho. **From Linda's Diary**

We went back to North Carolina for the Bluegrass Festival. Spent some awkward time with the family. They were almost pleasant enough but there was this underlying ickiness (Linda's word) kinda like you're walking barefoot on a rug and you know there's a piece of glass in there somewhere.

I wanted my family to be happy for me, having built up five businesses, sold them, bought the Freedom Machine and was out there discovering the world.

But they weren't happy. They weren't even interested.

Tommy Howard

I don't think I'll ever have the words to tell you how much that hurt.

We couldn't get back to Mexico fast enough but we did make one quick stop at the border. Remember that locker Linda had stuck all of our valuables in so they wouldn't get stolen in Mexico? We emptied it.

Fifteen

The big destination was Mexico City but there was a stop or two along the way worth mentioning.

Manzanillo. The water there is warm (86 degrees) and the people are warmer. We met Harold, who is 70 and Holly, who is 60. Holly has a parrot named Peckerhead. Eats the leaves off every plant in sight and squawks like a banshee all the time but Harold and Holly, well, we put them on the Christmas card list.

> One morning I was taking an early morning Manzanillo jog and came up on a place I couldn't believe. The beach where the movie "10" was made starring Bo Derrick. Beautiful beyond words. The beach that is. Okay, Bo Derek, too. **From Tommy's Journal**

Guadalajara. Picked papayas and bananas right off the trees. One stalk of bananas was close to two feet long! That's a lot of banana pudding and banana bread.

Guanajuato. Drove through a two-mile stone tunnel coming into town. The whole town has a Spanish accent to it. Just walking around looking at it made me wish again that everyone everywhere could get themselves a motor home and get out and see what the world has waiting for them. Went to the Museum of the Mummies. Over a hundred mummified bodies from more than 150 years ago. They say because of the dry climate these mummies could last forever.

Spooky.

San Miguel de Allende. Beautiful and quaint at the same time. There's an artist on every corner. I called it the Laguna Beach of Mexico. We stopped to charge a battery for some strangers and blew our own battery to smithereens!

Lago de Guadalupe. Went to have a look at the Tula Ruins. There are some statues there called the Telamons of Tula. The fella that wrote *Chariots of the Gods* is pretty sure aliens from outer space built those Telamons. No argument here. Linda bought miniature replicas of all of 'em.

Mexico City. Made it. Fifteen million people and, it seems like, fifteen million cars, every one of 'em trying to pass the one in front. Had to modify the Winnie, in order to "fit in," no pun intended. Off with the rear bumper, in with the mirrors. It was still tighter than a size 8 trying to squeeze into a size 6.

Driving into Mexico City in a hailstorm - stones the size of marbles - and there's a telephone pole cemented upright in the middle of the road! Note to Tommy ... do not drive around here at night. **From Linda's Diary**

If you ever get this far into Mexico, and I sincerely hope you do, be sure to go look at the Pyramids of Sun and Moon in Teotihuacan where you walk down a main street called Avenue of the Dead because the mounds on either side look like tombs.

The best day in Mexico City was the day our friends, Chip and Susan Rains, flew in to join us on the Freedom Machine Tour for a couple of weeks. One of our favorite stops was Taxco, the "Silver Capital" of Mexico. We stayed at the Loma Linda Hotel (parking lot) overlooking the city where we could watch the town light up at night then fall asleep to the music of Mexican crickets. Seriously romantic. Waking up to the sounds of mules, roosters and pigs?

Not so romantic.

But it was a great two weeks with a great two friends. Hated to see them leave.

When you drive a vehicle into Mexico, you buy six month's worth of insurance from AAA. Our six months was about to expire but we were too busy watching cliff divers, going to bullfights in Acapulco and having shrimp dinners in our RV camp on the beach in Zihuatanejo to notice. If you plan on traveling south of the border and you're going to stay awhile, cut this paragraph out of the book and tape it to your visor.

Another thing: They are not big on warning signs in Mexico. We drove all the next day to get to Puerto Escondido only to find the bridge was out.

"Donde esta el puente?" I asked. "Where is the bridge?"

"El puente esta quebrado" the kid told me. "The bridge is broken."

It was dark by the time we got back to where we had started that morning. Didn't waste a day, really. More like we lost a day.

Oaxaca Indian women gather by the stream and do their laundry topless. Tommy felt it was his duty to point that out to me. **From Linda's Diary**

We were pretty close to Guatemala when we finally noticed that our vehicle insurance *and* our visas had expired. No problem, we'll just slide on down into Central America, get our insurance renewed and visas stamped.

Problem.

Tommy Howard

They wouldn't let us in.

If two frogs are in the bottom of a Mexican well twenty-one feet deep and they hop three feet and slide back two, how many hops will it take them to get out of the well and into Guatemala? That's what me and Linda felt like we were doing before we finally got our vehicle insurance renewed and our visas stamped.

Believe it or not, it was well worth it. No pun intended there.

From Top: Whale watching; Don't drive at night; On the Mazatlan beach; Tommy & Linda in the jungle.

Part Three

CENTRAL AMERICA

Sixteen

It was dark when we crossed the border into Guatemala and even darker by the time we pulled into what looked to be a safe place to park for the night. I couldn't wait to see what would be waiting for us in the morning.

Morning came and I couldn't believe what was waiting for us!

Outside the motor home was a whole new world of colors and smells and noises and animals and people pointing and talking a mile a minute.

Morning rush hour in Guatemala.

I almost wore out the camera before Linda was even awake.

The men were small – couldn't have been more than a hundred pounds soaking wet with their clothes on. The women all had pitch black hair, braided, and were dressed in blouses and skirts in more colors than a sky full of rainbows. A lot of them were barefoot.

Seemed like every man had heavy loads of fruits or vegetables or wood or logs or Lord knows what all on their back. The women had babies on their back and big baskets of anyone's guess balanced on their head. They were their own beast of burden and they were moving like they late to the party, leaning forward taking short, quick steps.

Like they were trotting.

I have tried doing it, but either you have to be born Guatemalan to be able to walk/troy like that or maybe I have just seen too many John Wayne movies.

We stayed parked there almost the whole day, taking in the parade, sure that they were looking back at us with every bit as much curiosity.

Quetzaltenango was the name of the town and it was just a taste of what was waiting for us along the rest of the nineteen thousand miles of Pan American Highway.

Next stop on the Freedom Machine Tour – Lake Atitlan, surrounded by five semi-active volcanoes and so full of so much to see and do it became our home for the next five weeks.

There's a nice little town on the northeast shore of the lake – Panajachel – with lots of good restaurants and markets. One day six local women brought the market to us, knocking on our door with armloads of merchandise. Linda bought fruits and sash belts for her and shirts for me. Made me think of our friend, Don Jones, the surfer back in Matanchen Bay with only two shirts. I almost sent him one of my old ones.

Organized all my costume jewelry and sold a bunch of it at the Gringo Market. Made $33! I'm a natural born haggler. Tommy said it was my blue eyes and blond hair. **From Linda's Diary**

We went picking mushrooms, we went fishing, we went sightseeing around the lake with our new friend, Arthur, in his inflatable boat and we went for a lot of walks. Day and night, we walked, no trotting, just soaking in the people, the lake, the sunrise, the sunset, the mountains. We didn't say it but I know we were both thinking it … wish we could share this with everyone.

Seventeen

A Guatemalan cat had kittens. Along comes a mean looking dog, licking his chops. The daddy cat hid around a corner and started barking like the meanest junkyard dog in Central America. Scared that chops-licking dog right out of the neighborhood. The mama cat looks down at her kittens and says; "Now you know the importance of learning a second language."

We had to learn Spanish.

Come to find out there was a school in Antigua, about sixty-five miles from our campground that taught Spanish by what they called the Immersion Method. We had to live with a Guatemalan family in their house and the only language spoken would be Spanish. We lasted one night. Just wasn't comfortable being out of the Freedom Machine. But we did go to the classes five days a week, seven hours a day for three weeks. We learned a lot but still had a lot to learn.

In more ways than one.

Eighteen

I met a young German back packer in Spanish class who had decided to walk from the Panama Canal to the USA. We quickly became friends and found out that while he liked to walk and we liked to ride, we did have one Guatemalan thing in common … we were both fascinated by one of the inactive volcanoes - Volcan de Agua.

We decided to climb it.

Linda declined.

Germany and me started out in the Winnebago heading for Santa Maria de Jesus, an Indian village at the base of the volcano. Why not drive as far as we could before the road ran out and the actual hiking began? As we were driving we came up on about a dozen Indians walking alongside the road. One spoke a little Spanish and, after giving us directions to the village, he asked if he and his tribe buddies could ride with us.

"Well sure. Climb aboard!"

We forded streams, pushed low hanging tree limbs out of the way (the ones we couldn't dodge) and forged our way deep into the most densely wooded jungle area the German and me had ever been in. Somewhere in that jungle we rounded a curve and almost ran up on two young boys walking the same direction we were driving. When they looked back and saw the motor home full of their own kind they dropped the load of wood they were carrying and took off through the woods like they'd seen a busload of ghosts.

The Indians riding with us thought it was hilarious. They called to them boys to come out of hiding and ride with us but they weren't budging.
I got out and moved their backpacks of wood and we moved on.

I have often wondered what those two boys thought they were seeing when they saw us coming up behind them? A chariot from heaven gathering up Indians? I'll never know. And I'll never know what the other Indians were saying when they all got off, but one thing I do know - we solid made their day. Probably the most exciting thing that had ever happened to them. They're probably still talking about it.

We pulled into Santa Maria de Jesus and parked the Freedom Machine in what looked to be a church parking lot. If your vehicle is not safe in a church parking lot where is it safe?

"Oh my God, look outside!"

We were surrounded, Must have been over a hundred Indians standing and staring at us the same way those two boys back on the trail did.

Maybe I should have felt threatened but I didn't. They were keeping their distance, fifteen or twenty feet back, just looking. Staring, actually, the way we would stare at a flying saucer if it landed in our backyard.

All of a sudden – BOOM! Thunder from the gods. The ground shook, the skies opened up and the rain came pouring down. Now when I say rain, in the jungle, I mean *rain*. Noah's ark kinda rain. Those Indians scattered like cats in a dog pound. Poof! They were gone.

We thought.

Tommy Howard

A few minutes later there they were again. With umbrellas. Not the type of umbrella you see city folk running around with, but big, and I mean big, banana leaves - holding them over their heads and I'll tell you what, I think they were working better than any umbrella you could buy in a store.

They stared at us awhile longer and then, figuring we weren't any kind of threat (I guess) they disappeared into the rain.

The volcano was still there, though.

When a mountain looks high and hard to climb, it usually is. Volcan de Agua, looked high and hard to climb. The trail starts at a cemetery so if you're the superstitious type you should probably stop right there. They say it takes four or five hours to reach the peak and another four or five to get back to the cemetery. Germany and me started climbing at about 3:00 am and got back that night. We passed by cornfields and coffee fields, we went through climate changes – from tropical to desert and the altitude gave a whole new meaning to the word breathless.

But we made it.

To the top and back.

Not only were we exhausted, we looked like a pair of cats – big cats – had mistaken us for scratching posts. It took over a week for the scrapes and scratches and bruises and bumps to go away.

Was it worth it?

Yes.

Would I do it again?

Absolutely not!

Nineteen

Sidewalks south of the border are very narrow, very steep, full of holes, cracks, raised sections, lowered sections and overhanging trees. Windowsills sticking at least a foot over the sidewalk are a concussion waiting to happen and pieces of metal are sticking up out of the sidewalk waiting to trip you. They should be named booby trap walks. All in all, one is much better off to walk in the streets and take their chances of getting run over.

From Linda's Diary

Twenty

Lake Amatitlan is beautiful and tranquillo. Lots of good restaurants with interesting foods. There's a vegetable here called huisquil, a cross between a baked potato and a boiled peanut. Interesting.

A group of young boys came to the Winnie and played songs for us. We recorded them. A little later, four men came by with trumpet, accordion, guitar and bass. Our own private concerts. **From Linda's Diary**

Saw the Yankees win the World Series. It was in Spanish but guess who spoke pretty decent Spanish by then? **From Tommy's Journal**

"Well, hon, our visas are about to expire here in Guatemala, so which direction shall we go? We're closer to El Salvador than Mexico. Not sure what's there, but we can at least go across the border and take a peek. "

Twenty-One

E very time we cross a border we know that what's behind us is behind us and what's in front of us is another part of this unimagined journey. Today, it was Guatemala behind us, El Salvador in front of us. Or, coffee, sugar, hemp and essential oils behind us, corn, rice, beans and cotton in front of us.

Plus a smoking volcano.

Real smoke coming from that baby. Flat got my attention. El Salvador means *Holy Savior*. That day I was calling it Holy Smokes.

"You come down to visit Cerro Verde? " asked the border guard.

"Never heard of it," I said, "What's a Cerro Verde?"

"One of the highest mountains in El Salvador, with a volcano beside it and a campground and hotel on top of it."

Is the volcano active, is what I wanna know?"

"Years ago, yes, but no more. Smokes and kicks up a little but that's what makes it interesting. You can look down from the top of the mountain and see right inside the volcano."

I had never camped where I could see down into a volcano so we'd surely do that. Maybe not that day, maybe not the next. That was how we rolled … here today, somewhere tomorrow.

But we'd get there.

We spent a night on the beach in Acajutla, looked around Sonsonate and La Libertad the next day but they were too hot for us so we went to San Salvatore and stayed the night at the Metrosur shopping center. Parking lot that is. Strangest thing we saw in all of that was a McDonald's and a Hardees restaurant.

Okay, let's go take a look at this Cerro Verde national Park.

Breathtaking!

Majestic!

Snuggled in like a cat on your lap between three volcanoes, surrounded by a jungle overflowing with plants and creatures you'd have to see to believe. Even the bushes were all trimmed up into the shapes of birds and animals.

We stayed at the Hotel de la Montana (one of the fanciest parking lots we'd ever set up camp in), a four star beauty sitting 6,662 feet above the clouds and yes, indeed, you could look down into the Izalco volcano. The natives called it the Lighthouse of the Pacific because back when it was active you could see the fire spitting out of it from way off on the Pacific.

Just when I thought the bizarre and unusual were getting to be commonplace with us, out come the biggest bats I have ever seen in my life, flying all around like a scene out of an Indiana Jones movie. **From Tommy's Journal**

We watch the sun go down through a forest of clouds then look down and see the clouds light up from underneath. I feel like a bird with a God's eye view. If I could save only one memory from this entire trip, sunset in Cerro Verde would be it. **From Linda's Diary**

I can't count how many times we both said, "First time I have ever seen that" or "Never saw such a thing in my life." Last thing we'd say every night before sleep was, "Wow! What a day! Can you believe what we saw today?"

We pretty much had the entire parking lot to ourselves, but one day a fella came knocking on the door asking to see inside the motor home. Even spoke English.

"Where are you going from here?"

"Not too sure."

I wasn't.

"Coast Rica is nice. It means rich coast and it is rich with beautiful beaches and wildlife, and Costa Ricans like Americans."

"Well," says Linda, "that's comforting."

"It is on the edge of the Amazon jungle. Have you ever heard of the Rain Forest?"

" Heard of it but, that is about all."

"Costa Rica rain forests are known as the jewels of the earth and since there is not a lot to do in Honduras or Nicaragua, why not go straight to where the jewels are?"

Tommy Howard

"Well, thank you. We'll consider that." I said.

We weren't in a hurry

Twenty-Two

The Pan American Highway is without a doubt the lifeline of the people. They walk on it, sit on it, lie on it, push carts on it, live beside it and nearly all the towns are along it. You get to see it all, too, because you'll be going about as slow as a plumber going for his tools. What do I mean by that? Well, best to say it *was* paved than to say it *is* paved.

Once we got used to driving slow, we almost liked it.

Like I said, we weren't in a hurry. In Hawaii they say "Same shirt. Different day." In the Freedom Machine we say, "Where are we? Here. Where are we going? There."

We drove about twenty-five miles into Honduras before setting up for the night at an ESSO station in a tiny junction village. Everybody was smiling and waving at us like we were movie stars.

Then it got out of hand.

About ten children came banging on our door trying to sell us drinks and tortillas. They wouldn't take no for an answer. We finally got them to lighten up when we threatened to call the police station, which happened to be right across the street. Would you believe they were back pounding on our door at the crack of dawn?

Time to move on.

Twenty-Three

Welcome to Nicaragua, country of lakes and volcanoes. We saw 'em both. Matter of fact, we saw two volcanoes *in* a lake, along with sharks and swordfish. Not something you see every day. 'Course, we were getting used to that.

Saw an oxcart being pulled by two goats. **From Linda's Diary**

Saw a man, connected to a pulley, walking at a 45-degree angle. Turned out he was pulling a bucket up out of a well. Must've been one big bucket. **From Tommy's Journal**

Twenty-Four

Costa Rica. Now *this* is the diamond country of Central America.

Stunning.

Everywhere.

Friendly.

Everyone.

I could live here.

Maybe one day I will.

We exchanged American dollars for Costa Rican currency and a little advice from a friendly banker …

"You must visit Cahuita. It is like a tropical postcard."

We took his advice and were glad we did. Cahuita is a nice little laid back village about 27 miles south of Puerto Limón nestled in the lap of tall coconut palms and beautiful beaches as calm as clamshells. We didn't see any campgrounds but no one objected when we parked right on the beach.

Wild first night, though.

Both of us were yanked out of a deep sleep to find ourselves bouncing around the motor home like two kernels in a corn popper! I moved the curtain back an inch or so and peeked out the window, like a kid peeking under the bed looking for the Boogeyman.

Nothing.

"Don't you dare go outside, Tommy!" Linda was terrified.

"Maybe that's their plan? To get us outside?"

We sat in the dark, not hanging on to each other – *clinging* to each other like Saran Wrap. Nothing happened for maybe twenty minutes so we figured it was safe to go back to bed.

Not back to sleep, though, for sure.

A few minutes later the motorhome and everything and everyone in it started rockin' again. I peeked out the window.

Nothing.

The third time it happened felt like it was coming from the front passenger side, so I lifted the curtain real slow and peeked out.

At a hog as big as life and twice as natural.

I had never been so happy to see a hog in my life. They don't have fences there so that ol' hog went roaming free, got an itch and found a motor home to scratch it on. Seen it hundreds of times back on the farm. Difference was, those farm hogs found a tree to scratch their itch.

We went back to bed. Laughed ourselves to sleep.

We spent the next night parked next to the pier. Lots of big scratching posts. Just in case.

Woke up to the roaring of Howler Monkeys. Their noise is a cross between a lion roaring, a basset hound howling and a cat with its tail being stepped on. Where's a rooster when you really want one? Or a hog? **From Linda's Diary**

Two weeks of R&R in a tropical paradise will do your soul good. Hated to leave but – the road was calling. We drove ten miles to La Boca, on the Gulf of Nicoya and spent a couple more lazy days lying in the sun watching the surfers and the pelicans floating around on the bay. If we closed our eyes and felt the sun and heard the surf we could almost be back at Mantanchen Bay. Man, if our old buddy, Don Jones, could see us now.

Twenty-Five

If you had told me during my years in North Carolina that one sunny day, on my birthday, I would wake up in a motor home parked on a cul-de- sac in San Jose, Costa Rica, I would have told you that you needed professional help.

But there I was – waking up on my birthday in the Freedom Machine, parked on a cul-de-sac in San Jose, Costa Rica.

With someone pounding on the door.

"You are parked in front of my house!"

"Yes, I hope that is alright with you. There are no campgrounds."

" Si si, is alright with me but how long you think you be here? I know a better place. I am the manager of a big country club, with much more room to park and much quieter than here. It is like a big park. With an Olympic size swimming pool."

"Well, senior, come on in. Lets have a cup of coffee. Sorry, didn't get your name."

"I am Sergio"

The Freedom Machine

We became good friends with Sergio; corresponded with him for years.

After about a week, he asked us, "Where you going next?"

"Wherever we end up, I guess. Got any suggestions?"

Si, si, I would go to Manwell, Antonio, for sure. Beautiful beach Only eight miles south of a little fishing village called Quepos. San Jose, here, is about half way between the east and west coast, so about one hundred fifty miles away. It is beautiful, if you like beaches, especially.

"You must see this area. Toucan Birds everywhere, monkeys, iguanas, sloths."

He stretched out his arm with his hand wide open.

"Let us say Quepos is here, at my elbow. You drive along toward my hand; the beach is along on your right, jungle on the left. Manwell Antonio is my hand, like a park, there are five different bays there."

He held up five fingers.

"Pacific coast tropical waters, low eighty's in temperature. North bay waters are pretty rough. Big waves come crashing in. Farther south bays are calm, smooth, peaceful, take your pick. There are trails that go through the jungle to the bays. They are about six feet wide but dark, even at day, because of the heavy tree top foliage. Like light at the end of the tunnel when you begin getting close to the beaches. So much light with the white sand and ocean waters. Some bays have big black rocks that turn red when millions of rock crabs totally cover the rocks. Jungle goes right down to the beach in some areas. Banana trees growing all along the edge of the water."

Tommy Howard

"Okay, Sergio, you silver tonged devil, you have talked us into it."

We spent a busy day in San Jose getting propane, groceries, hardware supplies, exit visas and pesos. Then, after one last quiet night in the parking lot, we were off.

The first eighty-five miles were easy going on the "paved" Pan American Highway, but once you leave the highway you won't see any pavement. You'll see dirt and rocks and rough going.

Being from North Carolina I have seen a few rain storms from time to time, but what we got caught in on a narrow dirt road, surrounded by jungle, was a little beyond the standards of any rainstorm I had ever seen.

We hadn't seen any traffic, even before the rains came and that had me wondering if we were on the right road. Speaking of which, the road began to disappear so we pulled off into a banana field to wait it out. Even though it sounded like we were parked under a waterfall we were pretty snug in our little cocoon of a motorhome.

"We'll just spend the night here and leave tomorrow morning."

With lightning flashing all around us, I could see outside. It looked like we were on a houseboat in the middle of a big lake. When I looked down and saw water seeping into the Winnie, I wished it *had* been a houseboat.

Fortunately the rains began to let up and by morning most of the water on the road and in the Winnie was gone. We started inching our way out but didn't get too far before we came up on an encampment of people milling around blocking the road.

" Que pasa?" I asked in my best Spanish accent.

"No bridge here. Water is usually low enough to drive through, but now is too swift and too deep. Maybe manana."

Manana turned out to be three days later but we felt right at home visiting with these people. They had no problem dealing with it, so why should we? They were content to sleep out under the stars. They found food, sang songs, told stories. It was like we were in a Boy Scout campground with a great opportunity to practice our Spanish.

Before we left each and every one of new friends there had been given the grand tour of the gringo's Casa Rodante. They were all fascinated. Never seen or heard of such a thing.

Twenty-Six

The Winnie was parked under the palms, the hammock was swaying under the palms and the ocean was waving at us from only fifty yards away.

We had bananas, papayas, oranges, so much fruit we became fruit-a-terians, and never felt better in our lives. Dick Gregory, who wrote "Cooking with Mother Nature", would have been proud of us.

Hogar dulce hogar. Home sweet home.

Manwell Antonio was everything Sergio had promised.

Jimmy Buffett, eat your heart out.

Twenty-Seven

Walking, swimming, walking, fishing, walking, eating, sleeping, dreaming it would never end. If I had been any more relaxed, I'd have been in a coma.

But mostly I was in a hammock, catching up on my reading between naps or just enjoying quiet times with my eyes closed letting the sun dance across my face. I had to buy another hammock to avoid strong daily conflicts between man and woman (aka Tommy and Linda). Much less expensive than a divorce for sure.

I've learned to live much more in the here and now. Not worrying about the imagined future. Not worrying about the past. Not trying to change anyone or anything. Living each day as it comes. **From Linda's Diary**

"I never saw anybody use a motor home like this!"

I looked up from the hammock and saw one of the biggest grins I had ever seen. Belonged to a man named Berlyn Temple, electrical engineer and businessman from Los Angeles.

"I've always thought of these things as a family hotel or a rolling bar at ball games and tailgating parties."

" Yeah, tis true, tis true. Most people buy, use and sell their RV without ever having a clue of what they really have their hands on, which is what I like to call a Freedom Machine, especially if you can figure out how to go full time."

"Sounds maybe like a good way to retire."

"No doubt about that, Berlyn. What people don't know is how economical it is. Why, $1,000 a month (Back in 1977. More like $2000 a month today. Still inexpensive) will get you anywhere you wanna be. Even in the USA.

"If you like nature, a campground in a national park will run you less than half of what a cheap motel room will run you. So much to do in these beautiful national and state parks and they are everywhere. Healthy living, too. I never met a national park that didn't have a thousand trails to hike. Heck of a beautiful way to spend a day.

"Eating in an RV is no more expensive than eating at home. Gonna, get me a microwave one of these days

"We don't pull a car. Tried that once, but why bother when a couple of bikes get us where we need to go and the exercise won't kill us either.

"Don't get a lot of miles to the gallon but believe it or not we spend less money on gasoline on the road than when we're at home, running around all over town. Full-timing in an RV, you just drift from one park or place to another and drop anchor for a few days or a few weeks – whatever your mood tells you. A tank of gas can last for months."

"Heck of a lifestyle for the money but tell me the truth, don't you get lonely for your friends and family?"

"Well, figuring that they'd rather be where we are than us being where they are, we give them an opportunity to come visit us anytime. We'll pick them up at the closest airport and when the visiting's done, let them off at the next one.

"You gotta look at what is real, what is important and that would be the time we have. Is it important to have all this fancy equipment and great big coaches they're making now? Hell, you can't even get 'em off the big main highways they are so heavy. And when you are traveling, enjoying nature and all there is to see and experience, how much room do you need?

"It is the travel, the adventure, the people you meet, the sights and sounds and smells and education that counts!"

Linda drifted by just as I was finishing up my sales pitch and threw in her two cents.

"Tommy's right. Why worry about a little quarter of an acre homestead with a mortgage when you can have the whole world for almost nothing? And, if you don't like your neighbors, just move."

"Another time to move is when the grass needs mowing." Berlyn was trying to be funny.

"Cheaper than owning a lawnmower, for sure." Says Linda, walking away.

Twenty-Eight

There's something about a wild mushroom.

Even to a pair of fruit-a-terians.

So, when Michael, our self-appointed guide, told us he could lead us to some of the best wild mushrooms in the jungle, we threw on our mushroom picking hats and followed him into the jungle.

The deep.

Dark.

Scary.

Jungle.

Sergio was right.

So was Michael. He led us to the mother lode of mushroom fields – a fool's paradise in a tropical paradise! We were like a couple of kids in a grown-up candy store.

Picking.

And picking.

And picking.

And then it got better.

"Follow me," said Michael, heading back into the jungle.

We followed and maybe a half hour later found ourselves on the banks of a river so regal it must have been created as a playground strictly for kings and gods.

We waded in it, we swam in it, we splashed around in it like, well, like a king and a queen.

"We must go back," Michael called. "It will be dark soon."

"Go ahead, we'll be right behind you."

We splashed around for maybe five more minutes then hit the trail we had seen Michael take.

Or was it that one?

Or that one?

"Michael?"

No answer.

"Michael??"

No answer.

"Well, how hard can it be, Linda? I bet any one of these trails will lead back to the camp so let's just pick one and mosey on home."

We moseyed.

And moseyed.

And moseyed.

Probably round in circles for about an hour.

"You know what, Tommy? Even if there was someone around to ask for directions, I bet you wouldn't ask!"

So much the good mood brought on by tasty mushrooms and regal rivers.

"Michael!!!"

Linda's voice carried real well in the jungle but it just didn't reach Michael.

We were lost.

In the jungle.

At night.

"Tell you what we're going to do, darlin'." I was trying to sound positive, like I'd been lost in the jungle a hundred times before and knew exactly what to do. "We're going to climb a tree and settle in for the night. In the morning, we'll start back toward the river and take a different trail and be home before you know it."

"We're going to sleep in a tree?"

The Freedom Machine

"Be cozy, don't you think?"

"Can snakes climb trees?"

I had visions of boa constrictors hanging from tree branches.

"Most of 'em can't."

"Michael!!!"

"Here!"

Do you believe that? All these searchlights suddenly came ripping through the jungle and, a few minutes later, there was Michael, leading a search party!

Lots of hugging and kissing and crying and not too long after we were back in our bed in the Freedom Machine, chewing on mushrooms.

"Woulda been fun to sleep in a tree, though, don't you think?"

She didn't answer.

Twenty-Nine

Adios, Manwell, Antonio.

It was like saying goodbye to an old friend. I'm still not sure what I would miss most – the natural beauty or the beautiful people.

Christmas was right around the corner and we'd promised the folks back home that we'd be there. We were a little too far south to drive back so we left the Freedom Machine with "Aduana" (Customs) in San Jose. It is mandatory that, if you *drive* in, your passport must be stamped *Con Auto* (with car). If you don't *drive out,* the government will assume you sold your vehicle and taxes will be due. You *can* leave your vehicle in the Customs warehouse though, which is what we did.

Fort Lauderdale, Newport, Greenville. So good to see family and friends! It was like a living Christmas card. **From Linda's Diary**

Hey, Daddy. I'm not going to talk at all about the places we've been and the wondrous things we've seen but ... Feliz Navidad! (I couldn't resist). **From Tommy's Journal**

Thirty

February 21st - back in the hammocks in Manwell, Antonio, recovering from the hustle and bustle and noise of the holidays. No noise here, unless you count the breeze in the trees, the water kissing the shore and the toucans putting on their afternoon concert.

Oh, and the sound of sipping pina coladas and pages turning. Linda was reading *Shogun*, I was half way through *Centennial*.

Those were the days, my friend.
We thought they'd never end.

Five weeks later, with our visa about to expire, we crossed the border into Panama.

Thirty-One

We hadn't been in Panama long enough to change our socks before it got a little political.

We were having dinner, shrimp langostino, when a couple of gentlemen sent over a bottle of wine with a request - could they join us after dinner? I raised my glass to acknowledge yes and sure enough, soon as they saw we were done eating, they joined us. It wasn't long after we exchanged how-do-you-do's that they got down to saying what was on their mind.

Simply and respectfully, they wanted us and the President and every American to know two things:

1. The people of Panama knew the canal was certainly no gift. In their opinion it was nothing but a rust bucket and they knew plans were already in the works to build a bigger one meaning theirs would be obsolete before it was even taken over.
2. The people of Panama were highly insulted that the Americans didn't think they were capable of even operating the canal.

From then on out every Central and South American country we visited had some sort of message we were to deliver to the President and people of the United States.

The Freedom Machine

We spent the night in San Carlos, about sixty miles from the "rust bucket" then moved on the next day to Panama City where we parked at the Hipodromo Race Track and took the train to Colón, at the Caribbean end of the Panama Canal. Can't tell you how strange it felt to be in the middle of a jungle and look up and see a boat the size of Manhattan coming through.

Speaking of boats, we got back to the city and moved the Freedom Machine onto the parking lot of Balboa Yacht Club, a fantastic place to meet a lot of interesting people, doing about the same thing we were doing, but with boats. Yeah, there were money people with big yachts but mostly there were regular good people with a sailboat and a dream to "Get out there!" The same debate would almost always ensue: which way is best, RV or boat? Both have their advantages so the final answer was do both.

You have not lived till you've seen the sun set over sailboats in the harbor. For just a split second they look like they've sprouted golden wings and are about to fly up into the clouds. Might make a nice little kid's storybook. **From Tommy's Journal**

Went to the races at Hipodromo. Lost $4. I could have bought 400 oranges in Panama City for $4. Really, they were a penny each! **From Linda's Diary**

Right around the time our folks were suggesting (strongly) that we point ourselves in the direction of home, we met a man with a ship that just so happened to be headed to Guayaquil, Ecuador. It also just so happened to be big enough to hold a motor home.

Well, well, well.

He told us that if we could figure how to get the motor home on his ship, and pay him a nominal fee ($3,000), he would transport the Freedom Machine to Ecuador where we could pick up the Pan American Highway and drive on down.

Tommy Howard

Well, well, well.

I was high as a kite! Wow, South America!

Little did I know.

**From Top: Trotters; Just another day on the PanAm; Lining up
to tour the Winnebago; Panama Canal. Bridge of the Americas in
background; Guatamalan Laundromat (yes, we did); Honduras
funeral procession; Follow the straight and narrow.**

Part Four

SOUTH AMERICA

Thirty-Two

We flew on ahead of Winnie and hung out in and around Guayaquil, Ecuador for about two weeks, waiting for the Santa Lucia to arrive with our home away from home.

We've seen no gringos and met only two people who speak English so Spanish would be the language we would be speaking, except to each other, from here on.
From Tommy's Journal

All the houses between Guayaquil and Quevedo are on stilts. The people use narrow boats to go from house to house or wade through waist deep water. This journey is like a living circus. New acts, new costumes, new customs. What a show! **From Linda's Diary**

The Freedom Machine arrived! It felt like our kid coming home for Christmas. Getting her out of port was a story for another day but most importantly she survived the trip with nothing missing, nothing broken, nothing bent.

And …

A representative from the Ecuador Pepsi-Cola Bottling Company offered us $45,000 for the Winnebago!

In the United States, we could have been lucky to get $4,500.

We said no thanks and got out of there before too many second thoughts could get the better of us.

On the road again.

Heading north toward Columbia but couldn't resist stopping in the little town of San Antonio de Ibarra, famous for its woodcarvings. I'll tell you what; these people know wood. They make them good ol' boy whittlers back home look like – well – good ol' boy whittlers. If you can make it out of wood, these Ecuadorians can make it. Beautifully!

We stayed at El Centro. Seems like every city or town, no matter how big or small, has an El Centro, a wannabe park in the center of town.

Ecuador was a lot like Guatemala; lots of Indians carrying all sorts of stuff on their back and head. They were trotters, too. It really looked strange to see an entire family, Dad leading the way, Mom next and then the children from large to smallest, trotting in line. If a family was large and the path was curved or crooked, it would look like a human snake rounding the curves. We could hear their bare feet on the sidewalks but nothing else. They never spoke as they trotted along, not even to each other.

These were small people, average male height about 5'-5'2", about one hundred pounds. The women averaged about ten percent less in size. They all dressed exactly alike. Men wore top hats, much like Lincoln wore only smaller. The men also wore beautiful grey, frock-like jackets, no arm outlets, with shiny bright silk underneath. The ladies wore colorful dresses, all hand-made or hand woven. The female children dressed like their mother, the boys like their father. I was told later that these "go to town garments" were kept in the families for years, and never used except for going to town.

What a beautiful, gentle people. So odd to see them so into cockfighting, which is legal here.

We watched as a wedding party threw rice over the bride and groom. When they had all left, a crippled old lady limped to where the rice still lay on the ground, got down on her hands and knees and started collecting it. Tommy walked over and gave her a bag of bananas and a basket of fruit. See why I love him? **From Linda's Diary**

Took us a couple of weeks but we finally decided to venture toward Mount Chimborazo, one of the world's highest inactive volcanoes. So high there was snow on the top.

"Whaaaaat! Snow? And look there, a road to the top! Gotta go up that road."

Big.

Big.

Big mistake.

The "road to the top" was for donkey carts, sheep, mules, cattle and people on foot. Winnebago's? They don't see a lot of them on that road, which would explain the dumbfounded looks we got as we drifted further and further off the Pan American Highway.

Houses in the low areas were all on stilts, high in the air. Seemed like a pretty inconvenient bit of architecture until we found out why.

"Most snakes can't climb."

Brought back images of boa constrictors hanging off tree limbs.

Our average speed was about five mph on the straightaway, down to three mph as we started climbing and laboring upward. About the time the air started getting chillier and the road started narrowing to less than the width of the Winnie, we had no choice but to turn around.

One problem.

No place to do that.

The only choice left was to back down the road until we could find a turn around point. Well, we'll just keep 'er snug to the guardrail and …

One problem.

No guardrail.

I've seen snails crawl faster than we crawled, backwards, inch by inch till we finally found a place where we could turn the motor home around. It looked a little muddy, but it was worth a try.

It almost worked.

We got turned most of the way around but just when we thought we were home free, the right side or downward side sank into mud so deep we could barely get the side door open. It was getting dark, it was already cold and no amount of digging was going to set us free. We were the new definition of "stuck".

We were not in danger of falling over and rolling down the mountain, but it was extremely difficult to be in the Winnie as long as it was listing at least thirty degrees. Got me thinking about them boys back at the Yacht Club and their sailboats. Would I want to be on the ocean in a sailboat listing thirty degrees or in a Winnebago listing thirty degrees on the side of a mountain?

I liked our odds better, even though there was little or no traffic on the road. A jeep came by, tried to help but it was like a David trying to tow a Goliath.

Still - miracles do happen.

Along came a big four-wheel drive truck, loaded with twenty- seven Indians. I didn't have to say a word. They all piled out of that truck and started digging, bringing logs, straw, anything they could find that might help give us traction to get up out of the mud. They also had a big, heavy chain that they connected one end to the truck, the other to the Winnie and, with Indians pushing and slipping and sliding, wheels spinning and mud flying, the Winnie was soon back on solid ground and level.

They all piled back into the truck, waved and smiled goodbye and disappeared round the bend.

Wouldn't take a single peso.

Thirty-Three

Spent some time in Laga Cuicocha near Otavalo then moved on to Atacames, a nice little beach town. Great camping near the ocean on the beach under the palms. Clean, pretty, safe and quiet.

No mud.

Discovered that Chilean white wine (that we bought in Ecuador) is the best in South America. Very mellow. **From Linda's Diary**

Linda made coconut ice cream from cream of coconut and milk and eggs. Delicious! **From Tommy's Journal**

The rains are starting to get us down. Time to head south to Peru and a dryer climate. Drove from Atacamus to Santo Domingo then on to Guayaquil and down to the Land of Sand. On the way, we passed this sign:

LATITUDE O.OO

"Hey wait a minute! We gotta go back and get a picture of that. We just crossed the **EQUATOR!**"

It was one of the few times we knew exactly where we were on the entire trip. (Don't know how that happened). We had lunch there to celebrate!

The Freedom Machine

A few hundred miles from the Peruvian border, we were already missing Ecuador. Hated to leave but then ... *we know what's behind us, can't wait to see what's in front of us.* We filled up with gas before crossing the border. It was eleven cents per gallon in Ecuador, $1.50 in Peru.

That wasn't the only surprise waiting for us.

Thirty-Four

We had the border crossing all to ourselves. No lines. No wonder. Within twenty miles, we were entering the Atacama Desert, six hundred miles of the driest spot on earth. By now, we had crossed enough borders to expect a lot of change, but going from the lush greenery of the Amazon Jungle to the empty barrenness of miles and miles of nothing but sand, sand and more sand was the most startling change yet.

Driving a little strip of broken, pot-holed asphalt kept our speed at around seven miles per hour. Let's see, only about fifteen hundred miles to Lima. Should make it in a month or two. I honestly now am amazed at how quickly we adapted to that speed without minding at all. Traffic? Barely any. Sometimes we would stop on the road, climb on top of the motor home, have a leisurely lunch and not see a single soul. We could have been the last two people on earth.

After staring at sand for hundreds of miles we came to an oasis … a fishing village called Zorritos. It was like going from one world into another; from a desert wasteland where the bones of too many creatures bore testament to the harsh reality of life (and death) on the sand, into a valley of every kind of green we could imagine, thriving with life. We parked next to an all night gas station near the beach and went and stuck our feet in the water.

A little later while I was busy doing some adjusting of this and that under the Winnie and Linda was busy sitting outside enjoying the peace, about half a dozen kids came and sat down not fifteen feet away. None of 'em said a word. Just sat there, staring. Maybe thirty minutes had slipped on by before one of 'em pointed to a bag of trash we'd left by the door and asked if they could have it. Sure.

They asked Linda to dump it near the beach where there was "old trash". She did and they dove into it like a pack of dogs, grabbing plastic bags, jars, paper and whatever else they found of "value". It got us to thinking that unless you witness it, you couldn't comprehend how certain people live so poorly, hand-to-mouth. Maybe "exist" is a better word?

We had a troubled sleep that night. Didn't help when the old woman scraping rice off the street sneaked into our dreams.

That was only the beginning of the "getting to know you". The next day while I was inside napping and Linda was at the table reading, the door swung open and in walked a couple of young girls come to have a look around. We learned right quick to keep the door locked at all times. We couldn't keep them from coming up, face pushed tight to the window, trying to see inside. Once while we were having lunch, I counted fifteen heads looking in. That was when we learned we had to keep the curtains drawn twenty-four seven.

They watch every move we make. All of 'em want to see inside the Winnie. I have seen them lined up twenty feet and more, waiting their turn. They were respectful and grateful when we shared with them. **From Tommy's Journal**

I asked a lady how long had it been since she had seen rain.

"Nunca"

Never.

She looked to be about fifty-something. Not only had she never seen rain in her lifetime, she told me that there are places in the Atacama Desert where there is no recorded rainfall. Ever.

In the village, the entire population would line up daily to get their water.

We're getting our water from the gas station. We have to boil it before drinking it or making ice. Too many people (unsuspecting travelers) running around with the "Inca Quickstep." **From Linda's Diary**

We hit the road for Lima.

I would walk among the stars long before we got there.

Thirty-Five

It happened somewhere in the Atacama.

Picture driving across the surface of the moon, alone, following the only road there is at about seven mph for days and days. That's what it was like driving across that desert. What was around the next bend? What was waiting at the end of "as far as the eye could see"?

No one there to tell you.

No one there to ask.

You had to go see for yourself. There was a Linda Ronstadt song we played constantly that helped us keep our sanity:

Send down some sunshine
And throw out your lifeline
And keep me from blowing away

I can hear it now. I'll be hearing it forever.

We usually tried to spend the night near someone's house or driveway or parking lot, whether they knew it or not. That night in the desert we were on our own. We felt safe enough. Besides the two of us, there was nothing around for miles and miles but miles and miles of sand.

Some time in the night I was pulled out of a sound sleep by a bright light outside and a voice inside telling me to go take a look.

Up.

I went out. I looked up. I could not believe how many stars were staring back at me, lighting the desert like a thousand angels glowing in the dark. Can't tell you why but I reached down and took a handful of sand. As I watched it trickle through my fingers I felt I had to climb to the top of the Winnebago.

Half lying, half leaning on the air conditioner, I was content to gaze at the magnificence of all that surrounded me. Hard to tell where the universe began and the sand ended. Hard to tell where *I* began and the universe ended. It was as if me and the stars and the sand and the universe were one.

Linda was asleep beneath me in the RV.

I was awake above her *on* the RV.

But not.

I closed my eyes and saw myself floating among those trillions of stars. I could have touched any one of them. I could have ridden a moonbeam all the way to the Andes and dropped from the sky on invisible skis and swooshed from peak to peak like an eagle flying free.

Out of my body or out of my mind?

"Oh, dear God, I know now what you meant the last time we communicated in Mexico and you told me I am a child of the universe. Thank you, I understand so much more now. I AM because I FEEL!"

"What do you feel?"

The Freedom Machine

"I feel that most people seem to think and live their existence as a dress rehearsal. Thoreau said, 'Let me be all, Oh Lord, except to be among the men who allow their lives to slip away into quiet desperation.'

Or even worse, live their entire life in the first center of consciousness; believing nothing is more important than making money. I am so thankful I left that center of consciousness in the Grand Canyon."

I opened my eyes. Looked at the stars. Trillions of them. Trillions of answers. How do I reduce those trillions to one, that I may be one with the universe?

Why am I here?

The answer was up there. A piece of a song called *Now* floated through my mind:

So hold this moment fast
And live and love as hard as you know how
And make this moment last
Because the best of times is now

The best of times is now.

The best of love is now.

The best of *me* is now!

Life is short. Live in the eternal now.

I stood on top of that RV, hand-in-hand with the universe, and sang:

The higher you climb, the more that you see
The more that you see, the less that you know

Tommy Howard

The less that you know, the more that you yearn
The more that you yearn, the higher you climb

The farther you reach, the more that you touch
The more that you touch, the fuller you feel
The fuller you feel, the less that you need
The less that you need, the farther you reach

Thank you, Dan Fogelberg. Play it at my funeral.

Thirty-Six

Two words describe Lima, Peru, when we got there.

Big.

Dangerous.

Francisco Morales Bermudez, President of Peru (in a coup d'état) had declared a 50% increase in the cost of food and gasoline. You can understand that the people, already poor as rats, were not pleased. They could riot all they wanted but when the smoke cleared they would still have "no hay derechos" - no rights against Military Rule.

Curfews were established. Anyone found outside after the warning siren sounded would be shot. If there were an emergency with someone needing to be taken to the hospital, the victim would have to be in a car, one person with a white flag walking in front, one in the rear. The lights had to be blinking and the horn blowing.

Lucky for us we had stumbled across a military person who gave us permission to park in a very nice restaurant parking lot. Of course one of the other military officers owned the restaurant so we had front row seats to all this midnight madness. **Nothing** moved all night except, every thirty minutes, we'd see and hear a chain of about ten to fifteen tanks, trucks and jeeps with gun torrents rumble by.

Come daylight, the siren gave the "You can come out now" signal. Six million people poured into the streets and life went on. If you can call it life.

Time to move on down the road while we can.

Machu Picchu sounded like a safe, far away place with a strange sounding name. We could drive to Cuzco, be "turistas" and shop our way through the open-air market buying handbags, goats and chickens before catching a train to the ruins.

The Freedom Machine wasn't big enough to hold Linda, me, goats and chickens so we stuck with handbags and headed for the train.

Whoops. Tracks were washed out.

We took a helicopter. Landed in a fogged-in Sacred Valley early in the morning with no one else around. They say there's a powerful healing energy comes out of the ruins. They also say that the original inhabitants were wiped out by a small pox epidemic. I wasn't sure if we were gonna be healed or run off by angry ghosts.

There was a lot about Peru that was, shall we say, unpleasant.

For both of us.

On the other hand, there was a lot that made us glad we made the trip:

The Ruins of Chan Chan. Not as spectacular as Machu Picchu but how can you not go see a city made of mud?

The Nazca Lines. Long lines, geometrical figures and giant drawings in the desert sand. From the air you can see the shapes of hummingbirds, spiders, monkeys, fish even human beings. When you figure that these shapes were drawn over 1500 years ago, you have to put them on your "Must See" list.

Went to see the Santa Catalina Monastery. Women would go in there (still do) when they were teenagers and live as nuns in total seclusion from the rest of the world. They would die in there! The place was a cross between a castle and a prison. **From Linda's Diary**

We felt so comfortable in Cuzco, we decided to set up camp there for a couple weeks. Every time Linda headed for that open-air market I must admit I half expected to see her coming home with a goat or a chicken. Once a North Carolina girl …

Thirty-Seven

"Whaaaat! A Winnebago in Peru?" I heard from the open window. "I can't believe my eyes! How in the hell did you get this thing here?"

His name was Johnny Dennis, businessman from Chicago.

After sharing a few glasses of Chilean wine and a few traveling adventure stories, including my "retirement" at 34, I knew what was coming next.

"How did you manage to retire at thirty-four?"

"Well, Johnny, I was lucky. I founded and developed five businesses in about ten years, but my biggest accomplishment was to know when to move on and, until I sold them, how to run the businesses in absentia."

"You mean, they were developed well enough to sell and retire at thirty-four, but you weren't even there?"

"Exactly."

"Now that is a trick I want to learn about."

**Editor's Note: Check the back of the book for Tommy's addendum, *Running Your Business in Absentia.*

Thirty-Eight

It can take an entire day to cross a border, but just remember these three little words ...siesta del gato.

Catnaps.

Sooner or later, the border guards will call your number and it will go something like this:

"Come on in, have a seat. Glass of wine? How many children do you have? How many dogs? Cats? Goats? Chickens?"

Etcetera.

In other words, make them your new best amigos. These people could cause a lot of trouble if they wanted to.

Linda just had a knack with these boys. I kept my mouth shut and watched the show. Boy, was she good! Within *minutes*, they loved her, and she loved them. Honestly in some cases everybody in the room would stop what they were doing and come be mesmerized by the blue-eyed blond in the Winnebago who just happened to be fluent in their language. I am telling you the truth, there were times they were blowing each other kisses as we drove off.

Tommy Howard

Our first stop, just twelve miles from the border, was the small seaside resort of Arica, also known as the City of Eternal Spring. It may have been the driest point on earth but throw in all that duty-free shopping, miles of beaches, volcanoes and the highest mountain lake in the world and we might just stay every day of those six-month visas tucked into our back pockets.

We had no sooner stopped than we saw a man and woman approaching us in a rather hurried manner. Uh-oh. Trouble already? Nope. They were rushing over to invite us stay in their yard.

"Right on the ocean," said he.

"And safe," said she.

We felt pretty good about that until they locked the gate behind us.

And they were never heard from again!

Turistas locos! We had a nice dinner with ocean front seats. Next thing we know, they're back, this time inviting us to join them for a drink in their restaurant - The Crippled Rooster.

Waiting for us were about twenty people, loaded with question after question. They acted as though we had driven all the way to Chile just to see them. Around midnight, the two exhausted guests of honor started saying their goodbyes when in came a line of servers and cooks pushing carts loaded with more food than you see on a Saturday night cruise!

Had we been set up? Were we about to get the bill from hell?

No. They wouldn't let us pay for a thing!

We finally staggered back to the Winnie about three am, feeling and probably looking like a pair of crippled roosters.

Next day, they were almost in tears to see us preparing to leave so we stayed with these lovely people for about a week. They just could not do enough for us. Finally when we did decide to leave the entire village turned out to see us off.

They were hugging and crying, we were hugging and crying and waving goodbye.

A couple of cars got in front and back of us, blowing horns and waving at the people who had come out on the streets to wave at us as we journeyed on. It was like a parade! After a few miles we stopped, hugged, cried some more and finally got out of town. I'll tell you what, with all the tears shed that day, Arica was no longer the driest point on earth.

We kept up with that couple for years via cards and letters.

Thirty-Nine

Everywhere we went in Chili, we were treated like royalty. The Winnie was packed with gifts, usually food, within a few weeks of us being there. Every day was Christmas Day.

What we appreciated even more was being treated with respect. No one ever came peeking in our windows hoping for a blue-eyed blond beauty sighting and no one ever walked in unannounced.

Another thing, and this took us awhile to figure out: wherever we went in Chile, we were asked the same two questions, over and over.

And over.

"What did you think of Chile before you got here?"

"What do you think of Chile now?"

Like I said, it took us awhile but we finally got it; the people of Chile were sincerely concerned that every last person in the United States thought Chileans were wild Indians, jumping around with feathers in their hair. They wanted us (Linda and me) to be sure to tell every last person in the United States that just wasn't true.

We told 'em we'd give it a go.

Forty

We drove south about a thousand miles to a place called Vina del Mar (Vineyard of the Sea) also known as the Garden City. It had a tropical atmosphere with all those miles and miles (seemed like) of white sand beach but those grand ol' colonial homes and tree-lined boulevards had us feeling like we were back home in the Carolinas.

There's a clock here in Vina, complete with chimes and music, made entirely out of flowers. Ask Tommy what time it was and he'd say time to stop and smell the flowers. **From Linda's Diary**

Linda asked one of the beautiful Vina women how she got her jeans to fit so tight. She said wash 'em, put 'em on wet, lie down and don't move till they're dry. Then stand 'em in a corner till you head into town. Believe me, they were snug! Wow! **From Tommy's Journal**

We made Vina del Mar our headquarters, venturing out on one adventure or another depending on the mood we were in. One of those venturing's found us skiing in Portillo, in the Andes. We found a parking spot – no charge - next to a hotel where rooms were $300.00 per night.

We skied for about a week and were packing it in when a Federally waved us down and wanted to know where we were going.

"We're heading to Santiago."

"Wait here."

He walked over and spoke with about six others same as him. Pointed at the RV several times then came back. I was sweating bullets by then. Turned out they were blanks. All he wanted was a lift back to Santiago.

"Would it be okay with you if me and my men rode with you to Santiago? Our ride won't come until tomorrow and we would like to leave today."

"Well, sure thing. Climb aboard."

So he and his six cohorts, rifles and all, piled in and waved us on. Linda and those Federalies had a ball for about five or six hours. I'm driving, they're all drinking Chilean wine and before long everybody, except the driver, was singing to the top of their voices, happy as fools in an outhouse.

It took at least an hour for everyone to hug everyone else and say their goodbyes. One of them was even crying he was so happy. And drunk.

That was another one of those nights when we fell asleep saying over and over, "What a day! What a day!"

Forty-One

We'd been waiting for weeks for money to be wired from our bank back in North Carolina and even longer for all the mail we'd heard was comin' our way. The day after our long goodbyes with the Federally boys the mail came in. No money, but, wow…mail! You can travel all you want and have all the adventures you want but getting mail from the folks back home ('Cept Daddy who always had more important things to do, not to mention he could neither read nor write) is like hearing your dog barking when you're on the last road to home.

We carried our postal treasures back to Vina del Mar and read letters and drank wine and ate popcorn till the middle of the night.

Forty-Two

A vicuña is a cross between a small llama and a camel and a kissing cousin to the alpaca. It has a cinnamon-colored coat softer than the best cashmere money can buy and warm enough to shield the animal from the freezing altitudes above 15,000 feet. Since you can only shear them every three years and since you have to catch them in the wild, an off-the-rack **vicuña** sport coat will run you at least $21,000. A made-to-measure suit *starts* at $40,000. A vicuña scarf? Some places get as much as $4,000.

What I'm saying is if you buy something made of **vicuña, it will cost you an arm and a leg. If you** *eat* **vicuña, it could cost you your life.**

I found that out the hard way.

Somewhere in the high Andes we came across a hole-in-the-wall eating establishment. Dirt floor, thatched roof, chickens, goats, bugs, anything that wandered in was welcome.

Including a couple of gringos from North Carolina.

Special of the Day? **Vicuña.**

"Well, when in Rome."

"This isn't Rome," Linda pointed out. "All the posters and information guides specifically warn of the dangers of **vicuña** meat and under no circumstances should foreigners eat it! Even the Spanish people who have lived here all their life don't eat it!"

"That's just for tourists and sissies visiting on some 10-day tour. We've been south of the border for three years now. We're almost natives. So, no problem."

Try as I might, I could not talk my lovely partner into even one little taste.

Thank God.

Less than an hour later Linda was driving the Winnie hard and fast over the most horrific roads (paths) peppered with the deepest craters known to mankind. I was in the back, doubled over in pain.

A lifetime later we got to the hospital. Linda ran to check me in, but after checking out the hospital she decided it would be more "hygienically responsible" to park the Freedom Machine in the hospital lot and have the doctors treat me there. The first two doctors through the door took one quick look and advised Linda to fly me back to the United States immediately.

"NOOOOOO!"

"Senor, what have you been eating?"

"Vicuña"

"Vicuña? Dios mio! It has such a high bacteria count that nobody except the Indians can eat **it and it has taken *their* digestive system** hundreds of years to adjust to it. Did you not read all the posters warning against it?"

"I tried to tell him, over and over again," said Linda, "but no, mister world traveler, smarty pants had to go against all the experts. He tried as hard as he could to get me to taste it - held it right to my lips and kept teasing me."

Here's where she did her best Tommy Howard impersonation.

"Just taste it. Don't be scared. It won't hurt you. Sissy, sissy."

Anyway, being as I had a good (but angry) nurse, and access to the hospital doctors, they commenced to try to save my life.

"You will eat nothing but white rice and burnt toast for a month." He looked me in the eyes on his way out and added, "If you live that long."

Comforting.

With me flat on my back and only able to lift my head no more than three inches, Nurse Linda had to become Miss Everything Linda; in charge of dumping, fetching water, finding propane, cleaning and all the little things that make an RV a home.

Plus, we were broke.

The money we were expecting by wire still had not come in and the government had changed hands in Chile, meaning, for whatever reason, our credit cards were no longer valid.

There's nothing more dangerous than a broke, hungry, blue-eyed blond with a husband about as useless as plugging a rat hole with an apple. I knew that. A local banker was about to know it, too.

The Freedom Machine

Linda strolls into a bank, finds the manager, a short, stout, okay fat, fella, backs him into a wall and proceeds to explain, loudly, how desperate we were. Whatever banking business was being done was all of a sudden on hold. Every eye and every ear was fixated on the tall, blue-eyed blond and the short, stout, okay fat, bank manger.

It was hungry woman versus stubborn banker.

No contest.

The blue-eyed blond cashed a $60 personal check from Greenville, North Carolina at a bank in Vina del Mar, Chile.

That's my girl!

Meanwhile, I was still dying.

It took about three weeks before I was able to walk, slowly. When our money finally arrived, I went to the bank to personally thank the banker. The minute we walked in, we were the center of attention. The banker invited us into his office and then invited us to have dinner with his family. We accepted on the condition they wouldn't be serving **vicuña** meat.

The doctors had not warned me about dessert.

It was a sweet macaroon of some kind and it threw me into a relapse so bad the entire family had to physically carry me back to the Winnie. I was shaking like an aspen leaf. Linda put me under five blankets, turned the heater on high and got on top of all that to keep me from shivering to death.

Freezing cold and sweating like a jug of ice water in the Atacma Desert.

Tommy Howard

Back to the hospital

The doctors and nurses couldn't believe it; worse this time than the last. They told us the sweet macaroon was the kiss of death because, with the infection still alive in my system, something as innocent as a macaroon could cause everything to fester (that was their medical terminology) out of control.

One of the doctors almost pleaded with us to go back to the United States for treatment because I was so weak he couldn't guarantee my immune system had what it would take to win the fight the second time around.

"If you stay here, senor, it may take two months to recuperate and, again, you may not live that long."

"I'm staying here, doc. Break out the plain white rice and burnt toast."

He then explained that I would have reoccurrences about every five years for the rest of my life.

'If you break a bone, it will actually grow back stronger, but an infection such as this permanently compromises the digestive system and upon occasions you will have a kickback."

As I am writing about this many years later, I can say he was not kidding. It hurts just to write about it.

Would I go back to Chile? I'd love to. Will I try **vicuña again? Never.**

Call me Sissy.

Forty-Three

If these chapters had titles, this one would be called TLC. Thanks to the TLC of Nurse Linda, I was starting to believe I might live a little longer than the doctors were thinking I would. I wouldn't have been surprised if they'd had a pool or a lottery of some kind – everyone in the hospital picking odds to see how long before the gringo met his Maker.

We drifted down the coast like a pair of Gypsies, stopping whenever and wherever the mood struck us.

Pichidanqui was nice and quiet. Good place to sit back, heal and watch the seagulls watching us. The ocean breeze was more like the ocean wind, though. Guess that's why there were so many windsurfers on the water.

Tongoy was warm, sandy beaches on both sides of the peninsula leading out to the ocean. One lazy afternoon we counted a dozen sea lions hanging out waiting for the sunset. Couldn't blame them, sunset that night was breathtaking

Bay of Coquimbo. We met an old fella from Kentucky who'd been in Chile twenty years. He said he'd been married four times and was going for lucky number five. Linda didn't say it, but I could read her mind.

"Lucky it isn't me."

And that was our life, drifting from town to town, resting and relaxing my way back to health. You might say I was on the road to recovery. The Grim Reaper had taken his best shot and I was still standing.

Little did I know he was waiting round the next bend in the road to have another go at me.

This time, he wanted Linda, too.

Forty-Four

Anybody with a brain the size of a pea has better sense than to be driving in the Andes Mountains with the day disappearing around them.

But there we were.

Driving through the Andes on the Pan American Highway, about five or six thousand miles from the USA, thinking we could make it to the next town before dark.

Might have made it if it hadn't been for the explosion.

Steam was all of a sudden billowing out from the engine cover shutting the engine down, turning the power steering and brakes into manual steering and brakes.

Houston, we have a problem.

We pulled as far off the highway as we could and took a look under the hood.

It wasn't pretty.

The fan blade had broken loose from the pulley and tore half way through the radiator.

"Okay, Mr. we-can-make-it-to-the-next-town-before-dark, here we are, on top of a mountain, no heater, no way to get anywhere and the nearest Triple A is maybe six thousand miles from here. Chances are the sun will rise tomorrow on two stone cold dead gringos. Any last thoughts?"

"Well, sweetheart, the good news is we are about ten miles from the next village and we just topped the mountain so all we have to do is put it in neutral and coast on down."

"Why didn't I think of that?" She slapped the side of her head. "We can probably coast right to the front door of an authorized Winnebago radiator shop with a full crew of experienced technicians waiting for us to take a number."

"Well, one thing for damn sure, we can't stay here. Now this rig weighs about seven tons and it's not going to be easy to manually brake but I think if we both buckle up real tight I can get her rolling and we can do this."

"What do you mean buckle up tight?"

"I mean sometimes after the road goes down, it goes up, so we gotta have enough speed going down to make it to the top of the next up."

"Good luck with that, Tommy. I believe I'll stay here and freeze to death."

Panic was maybe too strong a word to describe the look on her face. Slightly frightened look of concern would be closer to the truth. Anyway she found some sort of logic in the idea and climbed back into the Winnie. I believe I heard her mutter, 'Till death do us part' but I can't be certain.

We got the Winnie rolling but the road didn't go down too far before it went up. Ina heartbeat we went from 30 to 20 to 15 to 10 and the top was still maybe 100 yards away. We dropped to 5mph still 20 yards from the peak.

The Freedom Machine

"Come on, baby, you can make it!"

We were both screaming at Winnie, trying to convince her that she was the little Winnebago that could. I looked over to see Linda leaning back in her seat with both feet planted on the dash and pushing hard.

"What damn good is *that* going to do?!"

"Same damn good *that's* going to do!" she answered back, pointing at me standing straight up, white knuckling the steering wheel.

Four, three, two ...

"She's gonna make it! She's gonna make it!"

Made it!

At the beginning of this journey I had disabled the speedometer so I could practice the *Be Here Now* theory.

Eternal moment?

How about *last* moment? Because you are gonna die!

Can't stop now. I just gotta get up more speed going down so when another incline pops up we'll have enough speed to top it.

"Now, Linda, don't scream too loud cause I need to concentrate. Oh one more thing - the road's gonna get a little curvier so buckle up a little tighter, close your eyes and pray cause here we goooooo!"

"Oh, Lord!"

Tommy Howard

We started down, bouncing around like a couple of corncobs in a hay bailer. No power steering, no power brakes and, if we weren't buckled in tight, no Linda and no Tommy. We would have gone through the roof faster than a hound could clean out a bowl of gravy.

Off in the distance, we could see the village. Sleepy, unsuspecting, no idea of what was screaming their way.

Up! Down! Around the curves! Sometimes I swear the back rear wheels came up off the road and we were three wheeling around some of those curves. I didn't mention that to my wingman. Or would that be wing woman?

"Oh, my God, Tommy! We're going to make it! Look! A couple of houses! Let's stop here."

"Darlin', I've been standing on the brakes so long they smell like burnt outhouses. Best we can hope to do is cruise on off the shoulder into those weeds."

Just one problem.

The "shoulder" turned out to be a ditch full of weeds and now also full of a Winnebago. We didn't flip over, though, and there wasn't a drop of blood anywhere. Linda's face was as white as any sheep in New Zealand.

Okay, mine too.

"We made it, girl."

"We did, and now I would like to go to bed and sleep and wake up and find it was all a bad dream."

"Kinda tough going to bed when the Freedom Machine and everything in it is sitting in a ditch at a forty-five degree angle."

Barely got the words out before here comes a man with a big tractor. Seems a Winnebago racing down a mountainside and coming to rest in a ditch in Chile is the next best thing to a UFO landing in an Ohio cornfield. The neighbors come a running.

The man, Pedro, and his tractor hauled us out that ditch and into his yard. Oh, happy day! 'Course the next questions were how do we get the fan blade out of the radiator and where do we find a Winnebago Dodge 440 engine radiator? As Scarlett O'Hara said, 'I can't think about that right now. If I do, I'll go crazy. I'll think about that tomorrow.' Tonight, we were alive and Linda, Pedro, the neighbors and me all thought that was something to celebrate.

I fell asleep smiling and thinking, *happiness is a charged battery and a level place to park.*

Forty-Five

Daybreak did not wake us. Day crashing, smashing, banging and clanging like a drunk in a boiler room woke us.

Now what?!

I looked out to see no less than five men dismantling the front end of the Winnie trying to get the fan out of the radiator and the radiator out of the motor home. Took 'em a couple of hours but they did it, then tossed the pieces into the back of a pickup truck and headed out.

I went with them.

Little bit down the road we pulled up to what looked to be a barn. Inside that barn were what must have been a hundred old tractors and trucks in one state of dilapidation or another. Pedro's cousin came out, looked at what we had in the back of the pickup and said, "Follow me."

He walked into the barn and up to some tractor type vehicle about a million years old and yanked out its radiator. He looked around, walked over to another unrecognizable vehicle and pulled the fan out of its front end.

I followed him and the rest of them boys deeper into the barn where they commenced to beating and banging and shaping and molding such as I have never seen in my life, and I and my brothers have seen a lot of beating and banging and shaping and molding in the back of a barn. Just ask our daddy.

We took the "new" radiator and fan back to the Winnie and, after some more beating and banging, it fit like it was factory made. Never had a single problem with it the rest of the entire trip.

"Cuánto te debo? How much do I owe you?"

"Nada."

I could not convince them to take a single peso. But they did have two questions for me ...

"What did you think of Chile before you got here?" and "What do you think of Chile now?"

"I am solely convinced that Chile has the most beautiful mountains in the world and the best people on earth."

I meant every single word of it then and I mean every single word of it now.

Forty-Six

We tried to get an extension to stay in Chili another six months but the only way to do that was to drive back to Arica, a fifteen hundred mile round trip.

Adios, Chile. Argentina, here we come!

To get from Chile to Argentina we had to go over the Andes Mountains.

The higher we climbed up the harder the snow came down. Wasn't long before the road was impassable and traffic had to be diverted through a train tunnel. If a train can fit through there I was sure the Freedom Machine could, too. And it did. Rough ride, though. One would think there would have been some form of concrete, or dirt between the cross ties. One would be wrong.

One would also think that if cars, trucks and the rare Winnebago were being diverted through the train tunnel, the train would be diverted somewhere else. Or at least put on a delay of some kind. The consequences of thoughts like that tend to allow some people to get religion.

It took forever but we finally saw the light at the end of the tunnel and it wasn't a train. We pulled into the first open area we came to, closed our eyes and didn't open them for about ten hours.

The Freedom Machine

It is a feeling of peace that runs through me when I feel the breeze running through my hair, as it was the morning after our ride through the tunnel.

Until I wondered why, with all the doors and windows shut, would I be feeling the breeze in my hair?

The answer was because all that bouncing between railroad cross ties had shaken the Winnie so violently that the entire wall along the driver's side had split maybe three or four inches away from the floor which, in turn, had bowed a couple of inches in the middle. My college education wasn't of much use to me at that particular moment but growing up on a tobacco farm working with tractors and hay bailers and a daddy who said, "Fix it yourself" sure was. The Freedom Machine was tight as a tick in three days.

Some years down the road I would say, "Yes, nice trip, Wife lived in the Winnie and I lived under it." **From Tommy's Journal**

Forty-Seven

The road to Mendoza (once you're out of the mountains) might as well have been paved with gold. It was that good. Asphalt, divider lines and shoulders! We felt like we were on the highway to heaven. Could have been true because where we stayed our first night in Mendoza, a police academy, we felt like we were safe in the arms of angels. They just happened to be carrying rifles, not harps.

Next morning we woke to the sounds of a marching band and five hundred policías getting ready to parade. Guess who was parked dead center of their staging area? Motorcycles, dogs, horses, bayonets, rifles, machine guns and each division with its own style of marching paraded back and forth in front of us till we got dizzy. What a sight! Felt like the whole parade was just for us.

We heard they were giving free liquor at Cerro de la Gloria (The Hill of Glory), where the national monument of the Army of the Andes is located. Sounded like our kind of stopover and what a ride for poets and photographers! We drove through San Martín Park landscaped with water fountains, sculptures, manicured gardens, even a lake. Poets and photographers indeed!

We parked at the top of the hill, took ourselves out to lunch and then shopping and yes, they really were offering free drinks to the customers.

So far, Argentina was our kind of place.

Forty-Eight

The roads were better but driving in Mendoza was like nothing I had ever experienced. No Stop signs, no Yield signs, no lane dividers and no traffic lights. It was a free-for-all! Wasn't always that way. Seems some American engineers had been brought in to fix the problems. You know what they did? They put up some kind of lights at all the intersections for people to go on one color and stop on another. What a waste of money! I tried to explain, in my best Spanish, that if everyone obeyed the traffic signals there would be no more accidents and traffic would flow smoothly. They just gave me a collective blank stare and walked away.

My first driving lesson: I was driving at the breakneck speed of 35mph when I saw a big semi pull out to pass me. No way was he going to beat the oncoming traffic but instead of backing off and falling in behind me he just pulls over into my lane!

Once again it was Linda, Tommy and Winnie in the ditch.

Let's just say that how I was referring to the driver of that truck would not be found in the Book of Unconditional Love and Oneness.

My second driving lesson: We tried to always make it a point not to drive at night, but one night, there we were, cruising under the stars when all of a sudden a car coming toward us, turns **on** his lights. Thank God he was on his side of the road.

Tommy Howard

Linda: "Wow, Tommy, why is he driving with his lights off?"

Tommy: "Why are they *all* driving with their lights off?"

It looked like a string of lightning bugs coming down the road. We decided to play it safe and pulled off and parked in someone's yard till morning. I got up early to try and find anyone who could explain the mystery of the on again off again lights. I found a taxi driver.

"Senor, if you keep your lights on it will run the battery down."

In my best Spanish, I tried to explain that cars and trucks have alternators that keep the batteries charged. In his best Spanish he told me how silly that sounded because everyone knows it is gasoline that keeps the batteries charged.

Uncle!

Toured a very large Mendoza winery today. Bought some for Tommy. He seems frustrated with the Argentinian drivers. **From Linda's Diary**

Forty-Nine

The people of Chile wanted to know what the President and people of the United States thought of them. In Argentina, the people wanted us to know what they thought of us.

"Civil Rights are dangerous!" was something we heard more than a few times.

"Why do you say that?" was something we asked more than a few times.

"Simple. Let's say you have to stop for a train. There are no lights so someone is employed to stay there and stop traffic until the train passes. Civil Rights would give that employee the right to stop what he is doing, walk off the job and have lunch. Now there is no one there to stop the traffic when the train is coming. Think about how many people would get killed!"

Another example: We had met an upscale couple living in an upscale neighborhood but the roads in front of their homes were dirt roads. When it rained the dirt roads would become muddy swamps. No one could leave their property until the mud dried or until someone came to pull them out.

Linda: "Why don't you just pave the roads?"

Tommy Howard

"Because we value the lives of our children, unlike the Americans who build freeways in front of their houses where speeding cars could run over and kill their children and pets."

But it was still a beautiful country.

Fifty

We pulled up stakes in Mendoza and started the trek to Buenos Aires, the Paris of South America. Spent one windy night in San Luis watching the tumbleweeds tumble by. We named one of them Linda and one of them Tommy.

Spent the next night in Rufino taking pictures of the sunset.

Along the way we passed a lot of horses, wild ducks, game birds, sheep, hawks, herons, cranes, a lot of windmills and a lot of green, green grass. Pretty drive.

The Pampas are something to see. They're all over South America for about half a million miles. Kind of a cross between Kansas and the Everglades. If you stare at the landscape long enough it will hypnotize you. **From Linda's Diary**

We spent a day with friends in Ituzaingo, a suburb of Buenos Aires, doing laundry, washing the Freedom Machine, visiting. Around about midnight or so, we all went to a neighbor's kitchen (they used their kitchens as a living room) and watched the Ali/Spinks rematch. When Ali won, it seemed like all of Argentina went into an all night celebration.

Were those "Maybe it's time to settle down" feelings I was feeling tonight? Not sure. Still waiting for the answer to the question from my Grand Canyon experience. **From Tommy's Journal**

Called home. So good to talk with mom. I wonder if it's time to start thinking about a different lifestyle? **From Linda's Diary**

Fifty-One

When you see a sign that reads CAMPGROUND FOR CAMPERS you have to go see what's waiting, even if it's waiting somewhere down a dirt road.

The "dirt" was mostly clay so we relaxed a little but not enough to stop taking baby steps.

Thunder.

No problem.

Rain.

No problem.

Until the road started sinking.

We'd heard that during big rains it could take weeks before the road surfaced again.

Time to head for higher ground.

The good thing about clay roads is that the center is constructed a little higher so that water sheds off both sides much faster. The not-so-good thing is that when clay gets wet, it gets slippery. If I drove off-center the back end of the Winnie was either going to swing left or right with the next stop being our friend the ditch. We were holding our own till we came face-to-face with high water in a low road. The only way to get over to the other side and make it up the hill was to gun it, get up as much speed as we could and pray – not necessarily ion that order.

"Buckle up!"

"Oh, Lord! Here we go again!"

I figured I was about to break every spring the Winnie had under her but we made it back to the Pam American Highway. Upon inspection I was elated to find not one broken spring.

But there was something wrong with the steering.

Have you ever seen a cross-eyed Winnebago? The front suspension had been knocked so far out of alignment the front of the tires were facing each other. One of the tie rods was bent so badly, I had to take it off and beat it like a thief till it fit the way it should've.

If we ever meet, you and I dear reader, I will be happy to explain (and maybe brag a little) how to fix the alignment on a motor home with a piece of string and a small tree. Till then, take my word for it, before too long, we were driving the straight and narrow again.

Never did find the damn campground for campers.

Fifty-Two

We passed through Patagonia, a major tourist region at the southern end of South America then went on to San Carlos de Bariloche, known as the "American Switzerland". Also known as a one-time haven for Nazi war criminals and the place where I would meet my Waterloo.

It's a beautiful place – absolute magnificent vistas. Clear lakes surrounded by the snow-capped Patagonian Andes, Swiss chalet style homes, every kind of tree and flower we could imagine plus a bunch we could never imagine. Gorgeous. One of the highlights of our entire journey. We found a camping spot overlooking a 180-degree panoramic view.

My Waterloo was the power steering. It was leaking so badly I decided to take it apart and try to fix it. Why not? I'd figured out how to fix everything else these roads could throw at the Freedom Machine. Odds were in my favor when I tried to fix the power steering.

I tried.

And I tried.

Lord knows I tried. I did kinda sorta get it back together well enough to drive.

The Freedom Machine

If you can call trying to steer with something as loose as a grey goose and as stubborn as a team of jackasses well enough to drive. Gonna have to try getting it fixed in Buenos Aires.

A thousand miles away.

Fifty-Three

Holding that baby on the road was like trying to go sailing in an eggshell. That thousand-mile trip felt like two thousand before we finally limped back into Buenos Aires feeling as dead as a church on Monday.

Sleep, rest and a whole lot of doing nothing but nothing were the top three items on the wish list.

After we got the power steering fixed.

We met a fella named Roberto who had a friend named Ruben who took a crack at the power steering but no luck. Roberto and his wife, Susana, though, became our new best friends. We stayed in touch with them through Christmas cards and such and do you know, years later, they came to Fort Lauderdale and lived with us for a while. Roberto even came to work for me at a company I had started - Sundance Motorhomes. By that time I knew more about buying motorhomes, selling motorhomes and fixing motorhomes than anyone on the planet. What other kind of business would I have started?

Meanwhile, back in Buenos Aires ...

Lord have mercy, we found someone to fix the power steering! Now, how about that rest, relaxation and a whole lot of doing nothing but nothing?

I lay myself down and, like the bear said to the bunny as he disappeared into his cave for the winter, "Wake me when it's over."

Fifty-Four

We were pretty much at the southernmost tip of South America so, after several lazy days of getting the Freedom Machine and us road-ready again, we headed north toward Brazil.

The border guards would not let us into Paraguay. If they had, we wouldn't have gone around that little country and we probably would not have seen one of the seven natural wonders of the world.

Iguazu Falls.

I don't know how to describe Iguazu Falls. How do I describe driving out of a rain forest, which all by itself was like driving out of a postcard, and coming up close and personal with 275 waterfalls spread over a mile and a half? How do I describe falls taller than Niagara and four times as wide? Eleanor Roosevelt stood in front of Iguaza and said, "Poor Niagara." Linda and me stood in front of Iguazu watching that water fall in more directions than we knew existed and were speechless.

The falls were a dividing line between Brazil and Argentina, letting both countries stake a claim. We stayed a week, camped on the Argentina side.

One day we happened upon a group of people, all with binoculars, looking at a white-necked heron fishing on top of the falls. Turns out they were a bird watching group from The United States come to the best place in the world to observe birds.

"I don't remember seeing you on the plane coming over here," one of the tour ladies said to Linda.

"No, we drove our motorhome here."

"Motorhome? You can't get here by motor home. There is no road all the way here!"

As Linda was trying to explain her way out of what surely had to be a lie, this guy comes up with an amazed look on his face and says, "Folks, you are not going to believe this but I just saw a Winnebago Motorhome!!! How in the…?"

And Linda was saved from being the biggest liar in the jungle.

Fifty-Five

If you want to go from Argentina into Brazil by land, you have to start on the water.

On a ferryboat.

The big ferry that took people and vehicles across the river was in dry dock but there was a small barge transporting a few cars at a time. It looked like no more than a big raft. Would the Winnie fit? Maybe if no other cars were aboard? There was no turning back, so down the riverbank we went.

When the front wheels of the RV rolled onto the back of the barge, the front of the barge lifted out of the water like a horse rearing up. I kept inching ahead till the back wheels were on board then inched a little further till I was midway between the front and the back.

It worked.

We were level.

On a barge so weighted down we must have looked like a motorhome driving on water. People on both sides of the river were watching, holding their breath and praying, Linda and me right along with them.

"Dear Lord …"

A quarter of the way across.

"We know this is not the best idea we've had on this journey …"

Half way.

"But if You could find your way to …'

Three quarters. My body was so tense you could not have driven a wedge wood pinecone up my butt with a flaxseed maul.

"Give us one last push, we'd be mighty…"

Made it!

"Thankful."

Now all we had to do was get us off the barge.

"Linda, this could be tricky. You might want to watch and wait on shore."

"No dice. We'll go forward together or we'll go down together."

"Okay, darlin'. Buckle up."

"Oh, Lord!"

I knew as soon as the front wheels rolled from the barge to the bank the rest of the barge would surge up, meaning the Winnie would jack up like it was doin' a headstand.

By this time word had gotten around that some fool from the USA was going to do some sort of Evel Knievel stunt with a Winnebago. At least a hundred people had gathered, most of who had never even heard of a Winnebago – but every one of 'em with a free ticket to the show.

Full speed ahead.

The higher the front wheels went the lower the back end sank down (I had removed the rear bumper in Mexico City to reduce the size) till we looked like a hound dog dragging his butt across a cornfield.

Off came half the aluminum outside cover.

Those folks watching may not have known what a Winnebago was but they were sure getting a good look at what it was made of.

I was standing on the accelerator, Linda was pushing her feet through the dash and the crowd was cheering us on like the hometown soccer team. Some of the men rushed to join the party, throwing logs and anything else they could find under the wheels to help give us traction.

What a show! Smoke rolling up around us, the smell of something burning, wheels spinning, mud flying, logs flying and …

We made it!

Welcome to Brazil.

Or should I say The Amazon Jungle?

Wet and wild.

Over four million square miles of more "different" than you can wrap your imagination around: 40 000 different kinds of plants, 1,300 different kinds of birds, over 400 different kinds of amphibians, over 3,000 different kinds of fish and over 350 different kinds of reptiles. Now *that's* a different kind of wet and wild!

I told Linda to be on the lookout for the nearest wet and wild Winnebago jungle dealer.

"Aren't we supposed to get three wet and wild estimates to the insurance company first?"

Fifty-Six

Rio de Janeiro.

Wow!

We became big-eyed, camera toting tourists.

We stood in the shadows of Sugarloaf Mountain. We bowed in awe of the 125-foot statue of Jesus (officially called Christ the Redeemer) sharing His view of Rio from atop Corcovado Hill. We toured Tijuca, the world's largest urban rain forest.

We were tourists.

We visited Cascatinha Falls, Guanabara Bay and took a thousand pictures of Rio at night from the Dona Marta lookout.

We were tourists and what tourist doesn't take in a macumba and samba show? What tourist doesn't hit the beaches around Rio – as beautiful as any we'd seen and we'd seen plenty.

Finally, if you're a girl watcher, Rio is where you want to be. I found myself humming *The Girl From Ipanema*.

A lot.

Tommy Howard

When I was told that *Ipanema* translates into "stinky water", I stopped humming.

The Portuguese language can throw you. It may look a lot like Spanish on paper but when it's spoken, it's a language all its own. So much for all that Spanish we had mastered.

One of the last things we did in Rio was almost the last thing we did on earth.

We took a night tour of as many of the "you've gotta say you were here" clubs and then took a ride home on a tour bus with a driver in a hurry.

We were about five miles from home. The driver wanted to do it in five seconds. I figured he was a professional who knew what he was doing and was well trained in the art of safety first.

Until we noticed that when he took the curves on two wheels he would sit on the high side of his seat and lean his body into the turn as far as he could.

Now, I never was all that good at physics, but a 15 -ton bus is not going to be kept from flipping over by the driver leaning in **any** direction. Any fool in the world would know that.

So how come the two fools in the passenger seats were doing the same thing? I guess one will do all sorts of things when one thinks one is gonna die!

To this day I can not look at photos of Rio without seeing a tour bus racing through the streets full of three fools leaning as hard as they could into Dead Man's Curve.

I did not tip the driver.

Fifty-Seven

Time to head back to Buenos Aires.

The large ferry had been repaired by the time we got back to the river separating Brazil and Argentina so the crossing was almost boring, which was just fine with us.

But the gods of destruction weren't done with us yet.

Back in the Freedom Machine, about ten miles from Buenos Aires, right after one of us said, "Home free" we heard what sounded like a dozen Howler Monkeys caught up in the duel wheel suspension coming from the back of the Winnie.

Within seconds, smoke, dust, maybe a little gravel and the smell of burning rubber settled over the coach like a ghost over a graveyard.

What had happened was the cover between the wheels and the floor had come loose from the floor and fallen down on the rear wheels on the passenger side. I have to say that was one of my better fix-it jobs of the entire journey.

We had no sooner gotten back up to speed than this car pulls alongside with the driver frantically waving for us to stop.

I rolled down my window. The driver yells out, "Would you be interested in trading your Winnebago?"

Fifty-Eight

"What is the value of your Winnebago?"

"Believe it or not, we were offered $45,000 by the Ecuador Pepsi Cola Bottling Company."

"Done! We will trade!"

"For what?"

"Follow me, please?"

We followed him into a large barn and there sat about twenty-five of the most beautiful antique cars, all in new or like new condition.

"Pick out $45,000 worth of cars. You pay for shipping."

"Linda?"

"I want to go home, Tommy. It's been nearly four years."

"Well then, darlin', let's go car shopping."

We chose three: a 1937 Midnight Blue LaSalle, a 1932 Dodge Sedan, with running boards (An Al Capone car, candy apple red) and a 1925 convertible

Overland with original spokes, ooogah horn and brand new Argentinian leather interior.

We spent the night at his place. Next morning he drove us to the airport and, true to his word, he shipped the cars (we paid $10,000 shipping and picked them up in Newport News, Virginia, three months later.)

The plane ride back was uneventful.

Until we began our flight over the Atacama Desert.

I was half asleep, my head against the wall, looking down, remembering, then suddenly *seeing* a Winnebago way down there with some dreamer sitting on top gazing way up here – into the stars.

Why am I here?

The universe – God - told me the answer would come when I least expected it. I would know it was real. I would know without a shadow of a doubt it was the truth.

It seemed the airplane disappeared from around me and there I was, once again flying among the stars like I had envisioned that night in the desert, half sitting, and half lying on top of the Winnie.

Once again holding hands with God, the great I Am, the universe, whatever you choose to call it.

"Why are you here?"

"To give! I am here to give! Out of unconditional love and oneness. There can be no more rewarding experience than the *joy of giving*! The more I genuinely give with the sincere desire to help my fellow man, the more the happiness that will fold back into my life."

Tommy Howard

Tears fell.

My eyes blurred.

Why am I here? I had been told the answer would be a simple one. It had been in front of me since I was a kid growing up in North Carolina, following my Uncle Moses around. He was the greatest, most giving man I ever knew, living the truth of giving for all to see. To have known him was to have known the meaning of giving.

Why didn't I see it?

What took me so long?

The plane flew on. What now? What next?

Maybe back to the Grand Canyon to finish my conversation with the rock that has been there for four and a half million years. I'll find it. It'll look the same. I will, too.

On the outside.

Seems as though all my past inner fears and doubts and worries have been conquered. I'm not struggling to impress or boost my ego. No need to. I know who I am. And I'm happy being me. **From Linda's Diary**

From Top: Linda had me drive slowly across this bridge to give her more time to pray; Houses on stilts because snakes can't climb; Valparaiso, Chile; Busy highway; One of the better roads; Linda skiing in August. Portillo, Chile; Machu Picchu; The Equator; Iguazu Falls.

Closing Thoughts

W hat was the journey really like?

Incredible, unforgettable, exciting, fascinating, frightening and confusing.

Really?

Bewildering, entertaining, educating, enchanting, mystifying and revealing.

Truly?

Ridiculous, bizarre, absurd, frustrating, unorganized, lucky and lots of fun.

Several people who are considering taking this trip have contacted me. I tell them all the same thing. It will be all of the above.

Guaranteed.

If you do go, and have a wonderful experience, I want absolutely no credit. If you do go and don't "make it", I want absolutely no responsibility.

Addendum #1

First you have to know what is important in life.

Most business people I've met are on the trail of "The name of the game is profit!" Their life dwells there and everything else becomes unimportant. They put their whole heart and soul into it all day every day, make a few bucks and think they have mastered what is important in life.

At what cost and sacrifice?

They have a hard time accepting retirement and a harder time enjoying the things in life that really matter, because none of that was ever important to them.

My theory:

The name of the game is P.F.

Personal Freedom.

In other words, YOU RUN THE BUSINESS. THE BUSINESS DOESN'T RUN YOU!

Actually, I was more or less forced into how to do this. I can't say what other people do. They, as do all of us, have a choice which, by the way, is the only thing that separates us from the animals.

We have a choice.

Let me give you an example:

A squirrel gets up every morning and starts foraging, looking for acorns, his food and security. You could put a million acorns around the tree, enough to last ten lifetimes, but to the squirrel, the name of the game is forage and hide and he will forage and hide until he dies.

He has no choice.

How much different is that from the businessperson that has to make that second million? That third million, that forth - locked into battling the almighty dollar till the Almighty takes them.

You are not a squirrel. You have a choice. When is enough, enough?

That's what separated me from everyone else in business. I found out early when enough was enough.

My favorite author, Ken Keyes Jr. (Handbook to Higher Consciousness) explains it perfectly.

It all comes down to what consciousness we choose to dwell in, and remember, we do have choices.

Security.

Sensation.

The Freedom Machine

Power.

Love.

Cornucopia.

Conscious Awareness.

Cosmic Consciousness

The people living only to make more money, more money, and more money choose the first, second, and third center of consciousness.

I choose the forth, fifth, sixth and seventh. The Grand Canyon Experience spelled it out for me ... *life is short, the world is big, what are you going to do with the rest of your life?*

Make a choice. Find the confidence to know when enough is enough.

But how? Let me give you a little background.

The first business I had was a heavy equipment construction business, a business my Dad had started but was out of control about the time I graduated from college. Triple bankruptcy is a better word for it.

His banker, lawyer, accountant and a few of his creditors approached me. The burden was put on me to take over and try to save the business or look the other way and let foreclosure begin the next day.

I had a choice.

I chose to give it a go.

Nobody promised me a rose garden but I could have gone to the Atacoma Desert and built a bicycle, chain and all, out of sand and ridden it to the moon easier than save that business. I thought college was rough, but it was a piece of cake compared to the trials, failures, frustrations and headaches that the following years would bring.

Bottom line is, I somehow pulled it out and made it work.

Then came the real challenge.

My wife decided she wanted to move back to Greenville, her home town and also the town where I went to college, about seventy miles down the road. I was ready to put Newport in my rear view mirror, too, but how do I move and keep a business running at the same time?

If I could teach someone how to keep Daddy's business alive and growing, I could pretty much become a ghost manager running the business in absentia. It would also free me up to pour everything I'd learned in putting that business back in the black into a new business of my own.

The solution is all in the accounting.

Forget about looking at accounting as something you have to do to make sure the records are straight and the least amount of taxes are paid. Stop thinking "Accounting" and start thinking "Management Accounting".

An airplane needs instruments to keep it on course, avoid mountains and storms, get it to where it's going on schedule and the right people to read those gauges and instruments. No different with a business.

If you have the proper gauges in place and the right people with the experience to read them, you don' t have to have your butt in the seat of the airplane.

Every legitimate business has an Association. Join it and, as soon as you can, get the financials that are available. Study them. Work out the national average. Then, design *your* financial statements to follow the same format as those of the Association (National) average.

Now compare your figures with the Association (National) average. Not only will you know how well you are doing, relatively speaking, but these percentages will pinpoint where the problems may lie.

What is important is these percentages are based on Gross Profit, but lets forget that and use the words "Available Income" because that is what it is. Lets not make this complicated.

Ever hear of the KISS principle?

KEEP

IT

SIMPLE

STUPID

In other words, most systems work best if they are kept simple rather than made complicated; therefore simplicity should be a key goal and unnecessary complexity should be avoided.

Truth is, when people have their butt in their chair every day, they don't think all these figures are necessary and therefore don't use, analyze, study and ponder the significance of each

So the facts are simple. You either know what you are doing or you don't. If you don't know these percentages then you don't really know what you are doing and are running your business by the seat of your pants. Maybe once upon a time there was a time you could do that, but not any more.

It absolutely amazes me all the time when I stop by to see a friend in the same business as I and find him so busy putting out fires and dealing with the immediate situation, he doesn't have time to P-L-A-N.

Lets look ay the national average (hypothetically) of a general rental business:

Equipment Not Returned.	2%
Uncollectable Debt	2%
Equipment Maintenance	6%

Plus office supplies, telephone, everything but sales and the average national net comes out at 4.3%.

Now, put your company's percentages alongside the national average over a twelve-month period. Any less is iffy, any more is overkill. I learned that from experience.

Suppose my manager has a 1% rate of equipment not returned. Is that good? No, it means he's missing rental opportunities by being too rigid in his rental policies and as a result, potential customers are going down the street to the competition. I would tell him to adjust his policies. Lighten up.

On the other hand, if his percentage of equipment not returned is say 3, 4 or higher it's time to give some feedback.

Mr. Manager, our percentage of equipment not returned is too high. Let's take the following action:

1. No out of state rentals. Litigation kills any reasonable collections cost.
2. Require larger deposits on larger items.
3. Institute better follow up procedures. Letter #1 Letter#2, Letter #3.
4. Incorporate more persistent follow up telephone calls
5. Let me know your own thoughts and suggestions on resolving the problem.

Watch the numbers for the next month or two and you'll know if you (a) need to come up with new strategies or (b) you need a new manager.

You can monitor all this from a Winnebago on the other side of the world.

One more example.

Equipment Maintenance cost: National Average - 6%.

Your average: 8%

Mr. Manager. Maintenance costs are out of control. Please take the following actions.

1. Lower the governing speed on the lawnmowers, keep the blades sharper; experiment. For example keep records on synthetic oil vs. regular oil.
2. Use larger air filters on all engines, especially the big air compressors.
3. Furnish two chains with all chain saws, and advise customer when and how to change them.
4. Have alignment checked on all tire mounted trucks, equipment, etc.
5. Give better usage instructions to customers. Have written instructions mounted on each piece of equipment. Keep them simple.
6. Let me know your thoughts and suggestions on how to reduce 8% by at least 2-3%.

You don't need to be on site to monitor know what's happening on a daily bases. The next two or three month's financials will tell you that.

I may be in Switzerland, when I send this letter. I may be in Chile. The point is, I *can* be in Switzerland or Chile, away from the distracting daily demands that can cause snap decisions I would live to regret. I can sit, study and decide, all from the comfort and quiet of my RV … running my business in absentia.

Making any sense? Any business can be run like this. If it can't find one that can.

Life is too short to do it any other way.

Addendum #2

I memorized these 12 Pathways in 1973 and continue to use them as my guide every day.

THE TWELVE PATHWAYS

TO THE HIGHER CONSCIOUSNESS PLANES OF UNCONDITIONAL LOVE AND ONENESS

Freeing Myself

1. I am freeing myself from security, sensation, and power addictions that make me try to forcefully control situations in my life, and thus destroy my serenity and keep me from loving myself and others.
2. I am discovering how my consciousness-dominating addictions create my illusory version of the changing world of people and situations around me.
3. I welcome the opportunity (even if painful) that my minute-to-minute experience offers me to become aware of the addictions I must reprogram to be liberated from my robot-like emotional patterns.

Being Here Now

4. I always remember that I have everything I need to enjoy my here and now, unless I am letting my consciousness be dominated by demands and expectations based on the dead past or the imagined future.
5. I take full responsibility here and now for everything I experience, for it is my own programming that creates my actions and also influences the reactions of people around me.
6. I accept myself completely here and now and consciously experience everything I feel, think, say, and do (including my emotion-backed addictions) as a necessary part of my growth into higher consciousness.

Interacting With Others

7. I open myself genuinely to all people by being willing to fully communicate my deepest feelings, since hiding in any degree keeps me stuck in my illusion of separateness from other people.
8. I feel with loving compassion the problems of others without getting caught up emotionally in their predicaments that are offering them messages they need for their growth.
9. I act freely when I am tuned in, centered, and loving, but if possible I avoid acting when I am emotionally upset and depriving myself of the wisdom that flows from love and expanded consciousness.

Discovering My Conscious Awareness

10. I am continually calming the restless scanning of my rational mind in order to perceive the finer energies that enable me to unitively merge with everything around me.
11. I am constantly aware of which of the Seven Centers of Consciousness I am using, and I feel my energy, perceptiveness, love and inner peace growing as I open all of the Centers of Consciousness.
12. I am perceiving everyone, including myself, as an awakening being who is here to claim his or her birthright to the higher consciousness planes of unconditional love and oneness.

(From: Handbook to Higher Consciousness/Ken Keyes, Jr.)

About The Author

There may be full time Rv'ers who have camped more than 15 years full time or visited more than 55 national parks, 49 states and 31 countries. There may be RV dealers who have sold more than 3,000 RV's. But only Tommy Howard has been on both sides of the desk and done it all.

Tommy Howard is America's foremost expert on recreational vehicles. He has bought more RV's, sold more RV's and repaired more RV's than anyone alive.

He is a full time RV'er; a rolling stone living wherever he decides to park for the night.

Made in the USA
Columbia, SC
27 April 2018